3 AB

THE
RIGHTS OF
TEACHERS

AN AMERICAN
CIVIL LIBERTIES
UNION HANDBOOK

THE
RIGHTS OF
TEACHERS
THE BASIC ACLU
GUIDE TO A TEACHER'S
CONSTITUTIONAL RIGHTS

David Rubin

General Editors of this series:
Norman Dorsen, *General Counsel*
Aryeh Neier, *Executive Director*

 **Richard W. Baron**
New York

40257

Acknowledgments

I would like to thank James Butler, Donald Conrad, Michael H. Gottesman, Stephen J. Pollak and Susan Ross for making comments and suggestions which were helpful to me in writing this book. I am also indebted to Robert Chanin, General Counsel of The National Education Association whose book *Protecting Teacher Rights, A Summary of Constitutional Developments* (1970) was valuable in suggesting an analytical framework for the subject matter. Harvey Smith provided indispensable assistance in source-checking the manuscript.

Dedication

This book is dedicated to my wife, Betty Ann,
whose insight and compassion have made her
an incomparable teacher for our children
and others fortunate enough to have
been her students.

Contents

Preface		ix
Introduction		11
I.	General Principles	13
II.	Freedom to Teach	24
III.	Freedom of Speech and Association Outside the Classroom	48
IV.	Freedom of Religion	105
V.	Freedom in Private Life	108
VI.	Freedom to Select Mode of Dress and Grooming	117
VII.	Freedom from Arbitrary or Discriminatory Action by School Officials	122
VIII.	Constitutional Protection of Procedural Rights	152
Conclusion		175
Selected Bibliography		175

Preface

This guide sets forth your constitutional rights under present law and offers suggestions on how you can protect your rights. It is one of a series of guidebooks published in cooperation with the American Civil Liberties Union on the rights of teachers, servicemen, mental patients, prisoners, students, criminal suspects, women, and the very poor.

The hope surrounding these publications is that Americans informed of their rights will be encouraged to exercise them. Through their exercise, rights are given life. If they are rarely used, they may be forgotten and violations may become routine.

This guide offers no assurances that your rights will be respected. The laws may change and, in some of the subjects covered in these pages, they change quite rapidly. An effort has been made to note those parts of the law where movement is taking place but it is not always possible to predict accurately when the law *will* change.

Even if the laws remain the same, interpretations of them by courts and administrative officials often vary. There are wide variations in the ways in which particular courts and administrative officials will interpret the same law at any given moment.

If you encounter what you consider to be a specific abuse of your rights you should seek legal assistance and endeavor to enlist the aid of your teacher organization. There are a number of other agencies that may help you, among them ACLU affiliate offices, but bear in mind that the ACLU is a limited purpose organization. In general, the rights that the ACLU defends are freedom of inquiry and expression; due process of law; equal protection of the laws; and privacy. The authors in this series have discussed other rights in these books (even though they sometimes fall outside the ACLU's usual concern) in order to provide as much guidance as possible.

These books have been planned as guides for the people directly affected: therefore the question and answer format. In some of these areas there are more detailed works available for "experts." These guides seek to raise the largest issues and inform the non-specialist of the basic law on the subject. The authors of the books are themselves specialists who understand the need for information at "street level."

No attorney can be an expert in every part of the law. If you encounter a specific legal problem in an area discussed in one of these guidebooks, show the book to your attorney. Of course, he will not be able to rely *exclusively* on the guidebook to provide you with adequate representation. But if he hasn't had a great deal of experience in the specific area, the guidebook can provide some helpful suggestions on how to proceed.

Norman Dorsen, General Counsel
American Civil Liberties Union

Aryeh Neier, Executive Director
American Civil Liberties Union

Introduction

This book deals with those rights which the Constitution of the United States confers upon teachers in their relationships with the public educational institutions which employ them. Although addressed to teachers at the elementary and secondary levels, the discussion is also relevant to the intimately related rights of teachers and professors at public community colleges, public four-year colleges, and state universities.

In recent years, the federal Constitution has emerged as a significant source of teachers' rights. Increasingly, the courts are affording protections to teachers on the basis of the First Amendment to the Constitution and the due process and equal protection clauses of the Fourteenth Amendment, among other constitutional provisions. It is the purpose of this book to describe, in a question-and-answer format, this burgeoning body of judicial decisions and to clarify for teachers and their employers the developing law.

The Constitution, of course, is not the only source of a teacher's rights. These rights are further defined by his individual contract, any relevant collective agreement, policies of his state and local boards of education, state and federal statutes, and state constitutional provisions. Teachers may, and often do, draw additional protection from these sources.

Since a teacher's rights may vary depending on the particular state laws, local rules and contractual provisions involved, as well as the interpretations which the courts in his jurisdiction have placed on federal constitutional or statutory provisions, the legal principles applicable to a teacher's problem may differ depending on the particular school district in which he is employed. In addition, virtually every case is unique in its facts. Furthermore, there are many cases pending in the courts involving the constitutional rights of teachers, and the law is rapidly developing and changing. Accordingly, this book is not designed to provide the answer to specific difficulties that a teacher may face, but rather as a general guide to developments in the law.

I. General Principles

(1.) May a teacher be dismissed, or his teaching certificate revoked, because he has exercised a right protected by the United States Constitution?

No. Although the nature and scope of a teacher's constitutional rights are not necessarily equivalent to those of a private citizen, a teacher may not be fired nor may his certificate be canceled because he has exercised a right which he does possess.

In an earlier era, the courts conceived of government employment as a "privilege" subject to whatever conditions the government wished to impose. This concept was reflected in the famous aphorism of Justice Holmes—speaking before the turn of the century as a justice on the supreme court of Massachusetts—who said that one "may have a constitutional right to talk politics, but he has no constitutional right to be a policeman."[1]

The same philosophy appears to have played a role in a 1952 decision of the United States Supreme Court upholding laws of New York providing for the elimination of "subversive persons" from the public schools.[2] Subsequently, however, the Court clearly rejected the "premise . . . that public employment, including academic employment, may be conditioned upon the surrender of constitutional rights which could not be abridged by direct government action."[3] "It is much too late to argue," the Supreme Court said in a more recent case, "that the State may impose upon the teachers in its schools any conditions

13

that it chooses, however restrictive they may be of constitutional guarantees."[4] As this book went to press, the Court, in *Perry* v. *Sindermann*,[5] unanimously reaffirmed these principles.

(2.) Can a school board constitutionally impose a sanction short of dismissal to punish a teacher for exercising a constitutional right?

No. A state may not condition the exercise of a constitutional right "by the exaction of a price."[6] Thus, any penalty which would make assertion of the constitutional right "costly" is forbidden.[7] Such prohibited penalties include, for example, denial of tenure,[8] refusal to promote,[9] suspension (with or without loss of pay),[10] reduction in rank or compensation,[11] denial of a salary raise,[12] involuntary transfer to a less desirable position,[13] denial of leave to attend professional meetings,[14] and reprimand.[15]

(3.) What if a school system takes no affirmative step to punish the teacher, but merely lets his annual contract expire?

The Supreme Court has ruled unanimously that a school system cannot refuse to re-employ a teacher because he has exercised a right secured by the Constitution.[16]

(4.) Can school officials forbid a teacher to engage in activity which is constitutionally protected and then punish him for insubordination when he disobeys?

No. "Insubordination can be rightfully predicated only upon a refusal to obey some order which a superior officer is entitled to give and entitled to have obeyed."[17] If school authorities cannot constitutionally penalize a teacher for a particular act, they cannot do so indirectly by banning the activity and punishing him for "insubordination" when he refuses to comply.[18]

(5.) Do these principles apply to nontenured as well as tenured teachers?

Yes. Lack of tenure or contract rights is irrelevant to the teacher's constitutional claim.[19]

(6.) What if a school board has two reasons for dismissing a teacher or refusing to renew his contract—one constitutionally impermissible, the other valid?

Several federal courts have indicated that the failure to renew the contract of a teacher is invalid if motivated in part by a constitutionally impermissible reason, even though the board has a valid reason as well.[20] Where a teacher's employment is terminated on both permissible and impermissible grounds, it would seem impossible to determine whether the board would have reached the same decision solely on the permissible ground.[21]

(7.) Does a teacher have a remedy if, because he has exercised a constitutional right, school officials force him to resign?

Yes. He is entitled to relief if he can show that he resigned "under pressure being applied because of the exercise of his constitutional rights."[22]

In a related field, the National Labor Relations Act prohibits employers from discharging employees for engaging in union activities. Some employers have sought to circumvent this ban by forcing the resignation of employees who have engaged in protected conduct. The courts and the National Labor Relations Board have repudiated this subterfuge, ruling that the employee has been "constructively discharged" and is entitled to reinstatement and back pay.[23]

(8.) May a school system refuse to hire a teacher-applicant because he has engaged in constitutionally protected activity?

No. As Justice Jackson once observed in a concurring opinion: "The fact that one may not have a legal right to get . . . a government post does not mean that he can be adjudged ineligible illegally."[24] Thus, where a teacher claimed that a public college refused to hire him in retalia-

tion for his testimony for the defense in a criminal obscenity trial, the court held that the complaint stated a claim
upon which relief could be granted.[25]

**(9.) May school officials punish or refuse to hire a
teacher for exercising a right secured by a federal statute?**

No. In one case, for example, a female probationary
teacher claimed that she was discharged because of her
absence from the classroom while serving on a federal jury.
A federal statute conferred upon women the privilege,
though not the duty, to serve as federal jurors. The court
ruled that the teacher could not be discharged for exercising
her privilege under the federal act.[26] It indicated that its
reasoning would apply equally to a teacher-applicant who
was denied employment because she exercised a federal
privilege.[27]

**(10.) What remedies are available to a teacher whose
employment has been terminated, or who has been disciplined, in violation of his constitutional or other federal
rights?**

The teacher has a remedy under the Civil Rights Act of
1871 (known as the "Civil Rights Act"), which makes the
responsible school officials liable in suits for injunctive
relief and damages.[28] Such suits may be brought in federal
court, but state courts also are obligated to enforce rights
created by the Federal Constitution.[29]

**(11.) What relief can be awarded under the Civil Rights
Act?**

Many teachers suing under the Civil Rights Act have
been awarded reinstatement and back pay less salary
earned in the interim.[30] Courts also have compensated
teachers for other provable financial injury,[31] and have
awarded monetary damages for loss of opportunity to
remain in or advance in a teaching career;[32] loss of professional status and reputation,[33] and physical or mental
suffering.[34] In recent years large damage awards predicated
upon factors such as these have been handed down by

federal judges—including one award of $20,000[35] and another exceeding $40,000.[36] In appropriate cases judgments for damages have been rendered against school officials as individuals.[37] And where bad faith has been shown, punitive damages have been awarded.[88]

In addition to awarding reinstatement and damages, courts can direct school officials to expunge from the teacher's personnel records any reference to the unlawful termination or discipline[39] and to refrain from communicating the fact of such termination or discipline to any school district or person.[40]

(12.) What types of specific losses suffered in connection with an unconstitutional dismissal or nonrenewal have been compensated by the courts?

Recently, a Washington state court concluded that a large number of teachers whose contracts were not renewed following a double bond levy failure were denied procedural rights under state law and the Federal Constitution.[41] Setting aside the nonrenewals, the court awarded damages for injury to the teachers' reputations, careers, and status in the teaching profession stemming from the use of subjective criteria in selecting the teachers whose employment was to be terminated, and for frustration, anxiety and mental suffering accompanying nonrenewal. In addition, the court compensated the teachers for specific losses, including the following:

— loss of salary because of the inability to find a similar teaching position;

— salary differentials between the teacher's former and new positions;

— cost of locating other employment, including postage, photocopying, long distance telephone calls, transcripts, mileage, newspaper subscriptions, required additional education courses, and updating of credentials;

— loss of benefits in the state retirement system caused by inability of the teacher to find other employment with an employer participating in the system;

— cost of obtaining medical insurance coverage equivalent to that supplied by the defendant school district to its employees;

— cost of medical expenses incurred which would have been paid by the defendant school district's medical insurance coverage had the teacher's employment not been terminated;

— cost of the sale of a residence in connection with a move to another locality in order to obtain other employment;

— cost of locating and moving the family to a new home, including a finder's fee on the new house;

— cost of additional transportation necessitated by driving to and from work in a more distant school system.

The court also awarded damages to compensate for a teacher's medical expenses, and pain and suffering, in connection with ulcerations of the colon and gastroenteritis caused by her nonrenewal; clothing expenditures which a teacher was required to make because of his new job as a salesman; loss of a wife's part-time job because the teacher needed to move to a new locality in order to obtain work or use the family car in his new employment; loss of wages in coming to court for trial; loss on the lease of a residence which the teacher was unable to sell; additional mileage costs in driving a child for orthodontic care in the new locality; the cost of a child's cello lessons in the new locality where such lessons previously had been received free; and restrictions on a teacher's social and private life where she obtained employment at a private school but was required to live in a dormitory at the school and care for and chaperone the students.[42]

While the court rejected the contention that suit under the Civil Rights Act could be brought in a state court, and the award of damages was not made under that Act, the purpose of the award was to compensate for injuries suffered as a result of the denial of federal constitutional rights as well as rights under state law, and comparable damages can be and have been awarded under the Civil Rights Act.[43]

(13.) Have courts awarded attorneys' fees to teachers who have successfully sued under the Civil Rights Act?

An increasing number of courts have awarded such fees to teachers prevailing in suits under the Act—both in cases involving racial discrimination[44] and cases in which other violations of a teacher's substantive or procedural constitutional rights have been shown.[45]

Although the Civil Rights Act contains no express provision for attorneys' fees, federal district courts have power, even in the absence of a statute so providing, to award such fees to the prevailing party.[46] Federal appellate courts have held that the award of attorneys' fees in civil rights litigation is appropriate where the actions of the defendants were "unreasonable and obdurately obstinate."[47]

Recent decisions, however, have suggested a broader standard. Several civil rights statutes enacted during the last decade contain express provisions stating that reasonable attorneys' fees may, in the court's discretion, be awarded to the prevailing party as part of the costs.[48] These statutes have been construed by the courts to mandate the award of counsel fees to a prevailing plaintiff "unless special circumstances render the award unjust."[49] This rule has been applied under at least one civil rights statute (42 U.S.C. §1982) containing no express provision for counsel fees,[50] and arguably applied to cases under the Civil Rights Act (42 U.S.C. §1983) as well.[51]

NOTES

1. *McAuliffe* v. *Mayor of New Bedford,* 155 Mass. 216, 220, 29 N.E. 517 (1892).
2. *Adler* v. *Board of Educ.,* 342 U.S. 485 (1952).
3. *Keyishian* v. *Board of Regents,* 385 U.S. 589, 605 (1967). *See also, e.g., Slochower* v. *Board of Higher Educ.,* 350 U.S. 551, 555 (1956).
4. *Epperson* v. *Arkansas,* 393 U.S. 97, 107 (1968).
5. 40 U.S.L.W. 5087, 5088 (U.S. June 29, 1972).
6. *Garrity* v. *New Jersey,* 385 U.S. 493, 500 (1967) and cases cited.

7. *See Spevack* v. *Klein,* 385 U.S. 511, 515 (1967).
8. *Pred* v. *Board of Public Instruction,* 415 F.2d 851 (5th Cir. 1969); *Tischler* v. *Board of Educ.,* 37 A.D. 2d 261, 323 N.Y.S. 2d 508 (1971).
9. *Orr* v. *Thorpe,* 427 F.2d 1129, 1131 (5th Cir. 1970).
10. *Puentes* v. *Board of Educ.,* 24 N.Y.2d 996, 250 N.E. 2d 232, 302 N.Y.S. 2d 824 (1969) (with pay); *Lafferty* v. *Carter,* 310 F.Supp. 465 (W.D. Wis. 1970) (without pay).
11. *See Finot* v. *Pasadena City Board of Educ.,* 250 Cal. App.2d 189, 58 Cal. Rptr. 520 (1968).
12. *Jervey* v. *Martin,* 336 F.Supp. 1350 (W.D. Va. 1972).
13. *Finot* v. *Pasadena City Board of Educ.,* 250 Cal. App. 2d 189, 58 Cal. Rptr. 520 (1968). *See Springton* v. *King,* 340 F.Supp. 314 (W.D. Va. 1972).
14. *Orr* v. *Thorpe,* 427 F.2d 1129, 1131 (5th Cir. 1970).
15. *Cf. Muller* v. *Conlisk,* 429 F.2d 901 (7th Cir. 1970).
16. *Perry* v. *Sindermann,* 40 U.S.L.W. 5087, 5088-89 (U.S. June 29, 1972). *See also Shelton* v. *Tucker,* 364 U.S. 479, 485-86 (1960); *Keyishian* v. *Board of Regents,* 385 U.S. 589, 605-06 (1967).
17. *Garvin* v. *Chambers,* 195 Cal. 212, 224, 232, P. 696, 701 (1924); *Parrish* v. *Civil Service Comm'n,* 66 Cal. 2d 260, 264, 57 Cal. Rptr. 623, 626, 425 P.2d 223, 226 (1967) and cases cited.
18. *Sindermann* v. *Perry,* 430 F.2d 939, 943 (5th Cir. 1970), *aff'd on other grounds,* 40 U.S.L.W. 5087 (U.S. June 29, 1972); *Parducci* v. *Rutland,* 316 F.Supp. 352, 358 (M.D. Ala. 1970); *Ramsey* v. *Hopkins,* 320 F.Supp. 477, 481 (M.D. Ala. 1970); *Stewart* v. *Pearce,* No. C-70 2441 RFP (N.D. Cal. Mar. 5, 1971). *But see Reed* v. *Board of Educ.,* 333 F.Supp. 816, 820 (E.D. Mo. 1971).
19. *Perry* v. *Sindermann,* 40 U.S.L.W. 5087, 5089 (U.S. June 29, 1972).
20. *Cook County College Teachers Union* v. *Byrd,* 456 F.2d 882, 888 (7th Cir. 1972); *Fluker* v. *Alabama State Board of Educ.,* 441 F.2d 201, 209, 210 (5th Cir. 1971); *Roth* v. *Board of Regents,* 310 F.Supp. 972, 982 (W.D. Wis. 1970), *aff'd,* 446 F.2d 806 (7th Cir. 1971), *rev'd on other grounds,* 40 U.S.L.W. 5079 (U.S. June 29, 1972); *Armstead* v. *Starkville Municipal Separate School District,* 331 F.Supp. 567, 571, 574 (N.D. Miss. 1971); *Montgomery* v. *White,* 320 F.Supp. 303, 305 (E.D. Tex. 1969). *See also NLRB* v. *Hanes Hosiery Division,* 413 F.2d 457, 458 (4th Cir. 1969); *NLRB* v. *Jamestown Sterling Corp.,* 211 F.2d 725, 726

(2d Cir. 1954); *Winchester Spinning Corp.* v. *NLRB*, 402 F.2d 299, 304 (4th Cir. 1968).

21. *But see Bekiaris* v. *Board of Educ.*, 6 Cal. 3d 575, 593 n. 12, 100 Cal. Rptr. 16, 27 n. 12, 493 P.2d 480, 491 n. 12 (1972) (applying test of whether teacher would have been dismissed absent exercise of constitutional right).

22. *Battle* v. *Mulholland*, 439 F.2d 321, 324 (5th Cir. 1971).

23. *NLRB* v. *Tennessee Packers*, 339 F.2d 203, 204 (6th Cir. 1964); *NLRB* v. *Saxe-Glassman Shoe Corp.*, 201 F.2d 238, 242-43 (1st Cir. 1953); *Baltimore Transit Co.*, 47 NLRB 109, 112 (1943); *Springfield Garment Manufacturing Co.*, 152 NLRB 1043, 1062 (1965).

24. *Joint Anti-Fascist Refugee Committee* v. *McGrath*, 341 U.S. 123, 185 (1951).

25. *Rainey* v. *Jackson State College*, 435 F.2d 1031 (5th Cir. 1970). *Cf. Torcaso* v. *Watkins*, 367 U.S. 488 (1961); *Scott* v. *Macy*, 349 F.2d 182, 183-84 (D.C. Cir. 1965).

26. *Bomar* v. *Keyes*, 162 F.2d 136 (2d Cir. 1947), *cert. denied*, 336 U.S. 909 (1949).

27. *Id.* at 139.

28. 42 U.S.C. §1983.

29. *Testa* v. *Katt*, 330 U.S. 386 (1947).

30. *See, e.g., Ramsey* v. *Hopkins*, 447 F.2d 128 (5th Cir. 1971) and cases cited.

31. *E.g., Armstead* v. *Starkville Municipal Separate School District*, 325 F.Supp. 560, 571 (N.D. Miss. 1971), *aff'd*, No. 71-2124 (5th Cir. June 9, 1972); *Lucia* v. *Duggan*, 303 F.Supp. 112, 119 (D. Mass. 1969).

32. *Sterzing* v. *Ft. Bend Independent School District*, Civil No. 69-H-319 (S.D. Tex. May 5, 1972); *Smith* v. *Losee*, Civil No. C-283-69 (D. Utah Jan. 27, 1972), 4 College Law Bull. 41 (1972).

33. *Sterzing* v. *Ft. Bend Independent School District*, Civil No. 69-H-319 (S.D. Tex. May 5, 1972); *Smith* v. *Losee*, Civil No. C-283-69 (D. Utah Jan. 27, 1972), 4 College Law Bull. 41 (1972).

34. *Lucia* v. *Duggan*, 303 F.Supp. 112, 119 (D. Mass. 1969) (pain and suffering connected with loss of weight and aggravated ulcer condition which were proximately caused by teacher's unlawful dismissal); *Sterzing* v. *Ft. Bend Independent School District*, Civil No. 69-H-319 (S.D. Tex. May 5, 1972) p. 19 (mental suffering).

35. *Sterzing* v. *Ft. Bend Independent School District*, Civil No. 69-H-319 (S.D. Tex. May 5, 1972) pp. 20-21.

36. *Smith* v. *Losee,* Civil No. C-283-69 (D. Utah Jan. 27, 1972) p. 8, 4 College Law Bull. 41 (1972).

37. *Lucia* v. *Duggan,* 303 F.Supp. 112, 113, 119 (D. Mass. 1969); *Callaway* v. *Kirkland,* 334 F.Supp. 1034, 1036 (N.D. Ga. 1971); *Smith* v. *Sessions,* Civil No. 1684 (S.D. Ga. Feb. 21, 1972) p. 4. *See Board of Trustees* v. *Davis,* 396 F.2d 730, 733-34 (8th Cir. 1968), *cert. denied,* 393 U.S. 962 (1968).

38. *Smith* v. *Losee,* Civil No. C-283-69 (D. Utah Jan. 27, 1972), 4 College Law Bull. 41 (1972); *Endicott* v. *Van Petten,* 330 F.Supp. 878, 886 (D. Kan. 1971).

39. *E.g., Parducci* v. *Rutland,* 316 F.Supp. 352, 358 (M.D. Ala. 1970); *Sterzing* v. *Ft. Bend Independent School District,* Civil No. 69-H-319 (S.D. Tex. May 5, 1972) p. 20.

40. *See Boyle* v. *Renton School District No. 403,* No. 740848 (Super. Ct. Wash., King County July 10, 1972) p. 28.

41. *Boyle* v. *Renton School District No. 403,* No. 740848 (Super. Ct. Wash., King County May 1, 1972) pp. 3-4, 6, 11.

42. *Boyle* v. *Renton School District No. 403,* No. 740848 (Super. Ct. Wash., King County July 10, 1972).

43. *See, e.g., Wall* v. *Stanly County Board of Educ.,* 378 F.2d 275, 278 (4th Cir. 1967); *Lucia* v. *Duggan,* 303 F.Supp. 112, 119 (D. Mass. 1969).

44. *E.g., Hegler* v. *Board of Educ.,* 447 F.2d 1078, 1081 (8th Cir. 1971); *Hill* v. *Franklin County Board of Educ.,* 390 F.2d 583, 585 (6th Cir. 1968); *Rolfe* v. *County Board of Educ.,* 282 F.Supp. 192, 201 (E.D. Tenn. 1966), *aff'd,* 391 F.2d 77 (6th Cir. 1968); *James* v. *Beaufort County Board of Educ.,* No. 680 (E.D.N.C. Nov. 11, 1971).

45. *E.g., Bates* v. *Hinds,* 334 F.Supp. 528, 533 (N.D. Tex. 1971); *Moore* v. *Knowles,* 333 F.Supp. 53, 58-59 (N.D. Tex. 1971); *Downs* v. *Conway School District,* 328 F.Supp. 338 (E.D. Ark. 1971); *Karstetter* v. *Evans,* Civil Action No. 7-573 (N.D. Tex. Dec. 6, 1971); *Caddell* v. *Johnson,* Civil No. CA-7-615 (N.D. Tex. June 30, 1972) p. 5; *Zimmerer* v. *Spencer,* Civil Action No. 69-H-804 (S.D. Tex. Mar. 24, 1972) p. 8; *Sterzing* v. *Ft. Bend Independent School District,* Civil No. 69-H-319 (S.D. Tex. May 5, 1972) p. 21.

46. *Sprague* v. *Ticonic National Bank,* 307 U.S. 161, 164-67 (1939).

47. *See, e.g., Williams* v. *Kimbrough,* 415 F.2d 874, 875 (5th Cir. 1969), *cert. denied,* 396 U.S. 1061 (1970); *Bradley* v.

GENERAL PRINCIPLES   23

School Board, 345 F.2d 310, 321 (4th Cir. 1965), vacated
on other grounds, 382 U.S. 103 (1965). The same language was used by the Fifth Circuit in Horton v. Lawrence
County Board of Educ., 449 F.2d 793, 793-94 (5th Cir.
1971). See also Rolax v. Atlantic Coast Line RR, 186 F.2d
473, 481 (4th Cir. 1950); Bell v. School Board, 321 F.2d
494, 500 (4th Cir. 1963).

48. See Titles II and VII of the Civil Rights Act of 1964, 42
U.S.C. § 2000a-3(b); 2000e-5(k).

49. Newman v. Piggie Park Enterprises, Inc., 390 U.S. 400,
402 (1968). See also, e.g., Miller v. Amusement Enterprises,
Inc., 426 F.2d. 534, 538-39 (5th Cir. 1970); Wooten v.
Moore, 400 F.2d 239, 242 (4th Cir. 1968), cert. denied,
393 U.S. 1083 (1969); Lea v. Cone Mills Corp., 438 F.2d
86, 88 (4th Cir. 1971); Robinson v. Lorillard Corp., 444
F.2d 791, 804 (4th Cir. 1971).

50. Lee v. Southern Home Sites Corp., 444 F.2d 143 (5th Cir.
1971).

51. The original enactment of §1983 in the Civil Rights Act
of 1871, 17 Stat. 13, expressly provided that proceedings
under that section shall be prosecuted in the federal courts
"with and subject to the same . . . remedies provided in
like cases in such courts, under the provisions of [the 1866
Civil Rights Act]" (emphasis added), Section 1 of which
became §1982. Thus, if the award of attorneys' fees is
warranted as a matter of course as a part of the effective
remedy in §1982 cases, it can be argued that the same
conclusion obtains in §1983 cases.

II. Freedom to Teach

The American notion of academic freedom stems in part from German concepts of freedom of inquiry and freedom to teach that characterized the German university in the nineteenth century. Under the German philosophy of freedom to teach, a professor was free to lecture on any subject and was not bound by a prescribed syllabus. While American theorists assimilated intact the idea of freedom of inquiry, they modified the concept of freedom to teach by recognizing the university's right to prescribe the general subject matter to be discussed by the teacher.[1]

The extent to which school authorities are constitutionally required to give teachers "freedom to teach" is a question which the courts have had difficulty answering. Many Supreme Court opinions contain sweeping language suggesting that teachers have broad constitutional rights of free speech in their classroom work. The Court has observed, for example, that academic freedom is "a special concern of the First Amendment, which does not tolerate laws that cast a pall of orthodoxy over the classroom."[2] Recalling the words of Judge Learned Hand, the Court said:

> The classroom is peculiarly the "marketplace of ideas." The Nation's future depends upon leaders trained through wide exposure to that robust exchange of ideas which discovers truth "out of a multitude of

24

tongues, [rather] than through any kind of authoritative selection."[3]

Thus, in *Sweezy* v. *New Hampshire*,[4] the Court suggested that teachers, at least at the college and university levels, have a First Amendment right to resist legislative scrutiny of their classroom conduct. In *Sweezy*, the New Hampshire Attorney General, authorized by the state legislature to investigate subversive activities, subpoenaed Sweezy and questioned him concerning his connections with the Progressive Party and the contents of lectures he had given at the state university. Sweezy refused to answer the questions on the ground that they intruded upon areas protected by the First Amendment, and was jailed for contempt. The United States Supreme Court reversed the conviction on the ground that the legislature had not authorized the Attorney General to ask the questions involved.

Six justices in *Sweezy*, however, felt that the contents of classroom lectures at public institutions of higher learning are shielded from exposure resulting from legislative inquiry. Chief Justice Warren, writing for a plurality of four justices, suggested that Sweezy had a First Amendment right to withhold the information sought. The Chief Justice agreed with the New Hampshire Supreme Court that Sweezy's "right to lecture" was a constitutionally protected freedom which had been abridged through the investigation.[5] The opinion broadly proclaimed that:

To impose any strait jacket upon the intellectual leaders in our colleges and universities would imperil the future of our Nation. No field of education is so thoroughly comprehended by man that new discoveries cannot yet be made. Particularly is that true in the social sciences, where few, if any, principles are accepted as absolutes. Scholarship cannot flourish in an atmosphere of suspicion and distrust. Teachers and students must always remain free to inquire, to study and to evaluate. . . .[6]

Although Sweezy taught at the university level, the considerations underlying the Court's concern about legislative intrusion into the classroom—that the free exchange of ideas would be inhibited by fear of the stigma of legislative inquiry and by excessive public scrutiny—also seem relevant at lower levels of education. As one federal court has said:

> Most writing on academic freedom has dealt with the universities. In *Sweezy* v. *State of New Hampshire* . . . for example, the Court spoke of the "essentiality of freedom in the community of American universities." Yet the effect of procedures which smother grade-school teachers cannot be ignored. An environment of free inquiry is necessary for the majority of students who do not go on to college; even those who go on to higher education will have acquired most of their working and thinking habits in grade and high school. Moreover, much of what was formerly taught in many colleges in the first year or so of undergraduate studies is now covered in the upper grades of good high schools. . . .
>
> The considerations which militate in favor of academic freedom—our historical commitment to free speech for all, the peculiar importance of academic inquiry to the progress of society, the need that both teacher and student operate in an atmosphere of open inquiry, feeling always free to challenge and improve established ideas—are relevant to elementary and secondary schools as well as to institutions of higher learning.[7]

Despite this broad language, the extent to which a teacher in a public school—or, for that matter, in a public college or university—has a constitutionally protected freedom to teach that is beyond the control of the state or the school authorities is unclear. In an early case, the Supreme Court held that a teacher in a *private* school had a constitutionally protected "right . . . to teach" under the due process clause of the Fourteenth Amendment—a right infringed by a state law forbidding the teaching of foreign languages in the first eight grades.[8] But the state has greater power to control the curriculum of a public school than a private school. In a public educational system, curricular decisions must be made by or under the aegis of some public body, such as a school board, which is democratically elected and accountable to the people.[9]

The power to prescribe the curriculum, however, does not necessarily mean that the state or a school board is constitutionally permitted to choose a single view of a given subject and command its teachers to avoid discussion of any other. In connection with the *Scopes* trial, William Jennings Bryan argued that the state had such power: "The right of free speech cannot be stretched as far as Professor Scopes is trying to stretch it. A man cannot demand a salary for saying what his employers do not want said and he cannot require his employers to furnish an audience to talk to, especially an audience of children or young people, when he wants to say what the parents do not want said."[10]

When the *Scopes* case reached the Tennessee Supreme Court, it ruled that the state could condition Scopes's public employment on whatever conditions it saw fit[11]—a doctrine that has been repudiated by the United States Supreme Court. But whether a teacher has any constitutional rights which he may exercise in the classroom, or whether, as Bryan contended, he is merely a "hired man" who has no measure of freedom to teach, has yet to be squarely faced by the high tribunal.

In a 1968 case in which one of the plaintiffs was a public-school biology teacher, the Court refused to decide whether an Arkansas "monkey" law, prohibiting consideration of evolutionary theory in a state-supported school, violated the teacher's constitutional rights.[12] Avoiding what it termed this "difficult terrain,"[13] the Court instead struck down the law on the ground that it was enacted for religious reasons and conflicted with the constitutional ban on establishment of a religion.[14] In a concurring opinion, Justice Black stated that he could not "imagine why a state is without power to withdraw from its curriculum any subject deemed too emotional and controversial for its public schools."[15] Nor was he "ready to hold that a person hired to teach school children takes with him into the classroom a constitutional right to teach sociological, economic, political or religious subjects that the school's managers do not want discussed."[16] But Justice Stewart, also concurring, took a different view: "It is one thing for a state to determine that 'the subject of higher mathematics, or astronomy, or biology' shall or shall not be included in its public school curriculum. It is quite another thing for a state to make it a criminal offense for a public school teacher so much as to mention the very existence of an entire system of respected human thought. That kind of criminal law, I think, would clearly impinge upon the guarantees of free communication contained in the First Amendment. . . ."[17]

Although the Supreme Court has not spoken authoritatively on the question, lower federal courts have begun to afford teachers a measure of classroom freedom within the parameters of their subject matter. Most of the decided cases have arisen in the context of demands upon teachers by school officials to refrain from controversial classroom discussion or assignments.[18] These decisions have eroded the vitality of a 1965 ruling rejecting the claim of a high-school teacher that the failure to renew his contract because he assigned *Brave New World* to his class violated his First Amendment right of free speech.[19]

(1.) What types of classroom utterances or assignments by a teacher have been held constitutionally protected?

The initial decisions involved classroom utterances or assignments by English teachers which school administrators, responding to the cries of outraged parents, deemed to exceed the bounds of propriety.

In one case,[20] a high-school teacher assigned for reading to his senior English class an article in the *Atlantic Monthly* magazine by a psychiatrist and medical-school professor. The article—a discussion of dissent, protest, radicalism, and revolt—contained repeated references to the word "mother-

fucker." The teacher discussed the article and the word, and
explained the word's origin and context and the reasons the
author had included it. Any student who found the assignment personally distasteful was given the option of having
an alternative one.

Asked by the school committee to agree not to use the
word again in the classroom, the teacher refused, where-
upon he was suspended and dismissal proceedings were
instituted against him. He brought suit under the Civil
Rights Act to enjoin the proceedings and appealed the
denial of preliminary relief.

The United States Court of Appeals reversed and directed the lower court to issue a preliminary injunction. The
court of appeals concluded that the article was "in no
sense pornographic," but was "scholarly, thoughtful and
thought-provoking," and that "[t]he single offending word,
although repeated a number of times, is not artificially
introduced, but, on the contrary, is important to the development of the thesis. . . ."[21] "[T]he question in this case,"
this court said, "is whether a teacher may, for demonstrated
educational purposes, quote a 'dirty' word currently used in
order to give special offense. . . ."[22] Accepting the conclusion of the trial court that "some measure of public regulation of classroom speech is inherent in every provision of
public education," the court of appeals expressed concern about "[t]he general chilling effect of permitting such
rigorous censorship"[23] and concluded that principles of academic freedom embodied in the Constitution barred the
teacher's dismissal.

In another case,[24] a high-school teacher in Montgomery,
Alabama, was dismissed for assigning to her eleventh-grade
English class "Welcome to the Monkey House"—a short
story and comic satire by Kurt Vonnegut, a prominent con-
temporary writer. The story contained several vulgar terms
and a reference to an act of rape. On the day following the
assignment, she was called to the principal's office for a conference with him and the associate superintendent, who
both expressed displeasure with the content of the story,
which they described as "literary garbage," and the "phil-

osophy" of the story, which they construed as condoning,
if not encouraging, "the killing off of elderly people and
free sex."[25] They also expressed concern over the fact that
three students had asked to be excused from the assignment
and several disgruntled parents had called to complain.
When the school officials admonished her not to teach the
story in any of her classes, she retorted that she was be-
wildered by their interpretation of the story, considered it
a good literary work, and felt that she had a professional
obligation to teach it. Upon her dismissal for "insubordination" she sought reinstatement and damages in federal
court.

In ruling for the teacher, the court stated that the first
question was whether the story was inappropriate reading
for high-school juniors. On this point, the court found
"nothing that would render it obscene" under criminal-
obscenity standards set forth in Supreme Court decisions.[26]
The court noted that the slang words were contained in
rhymes less ribald than those found in many of Shake-
speare's plays; that the reference to an act of rape was no
more descriptive than the rape scene in Pope's "Rape of the
Lock"; and that the anthology in which the story was published had been reviewed by several of the popular national
weekly magazines, none of which found the subject matter
of any of the stories to be offensive. It appeared to the
court, moreover, that the author, rather than advocating
the "killing off of old people," was satirizing the practice
to symbolize the increasing depersonalization of man in
society.[27]

The court also found that the conduct for which the
teacher was dismissed was not of such a character as to
"materially and substantially interfere" with reasonable
requirements of discipline in the school. Since the defendants failed to show either that the assignment was
inappropriate reading for high-school juniors, or that it
significantly disrupted the educational processes of the
school, the court concluded that the teacher's dismissal
constituted "an unwarranted invasion of her First Amendment right to academic freedom."[28]

(2.) Do these decisions confer blanket authority upon teachers to conduct their classes as they wish?

No. As one court of appeals has said: "[F]ree speech does not grant teachers a license to say or write in class whatever they may feel like. . . ." Rather, "the propriety of regulations or sanctions must depend on such circumstances as the age and sophistication of the students, the closeness of the relation between the specific technique used and some concededly valid educational objective, and the context and manner of presentation."[29]

In Lawrence, Massachusetts, an eleventh-grade English teacher, in the context of a discussion of the use of vulgar words whose traditional counterparts were socially acceptable, chalked on the blackboard the word "fuck," and asked if anyone could define it. One boy volunteered that the word meant "sexual intercourse." The teacher observed that the term "sexual intercourse" was socially acceptable, and the "word on the board" was not. "It is a taboo word." After discussing other aspects of taboos, the teacher went on to other matters.

The teacher was suspended and then dismissed on the charge of "conduct unbecoming a teacher." He brought suit challenging his dismissal on constitutional grounds. The court found that the topic of taboo words had a high degree of relevance to the proper teaching of eleventh-grade basic English, that the word "fuck" effectively illustrates how taboo words function, that eleventh-grade boys and girls have sufficient sophistication to treat the word from a serious educational viewpoint, that calling upon the class for a volunteer to define the word was a reasonable technique which avoided implicating anyone who did not wish to participate, and that the teacher had acted in good faith. The expert evidence differed over whether the teacher's use of the word was reasonable, appropriate, and conducive to a serious educational purpose. The evidence did not show the preponderant opinion in the teaching profession or in that part of the profession which taught English.

The trial court recognized that "[w]e do not confine academic freedom to conventional teachers or to those who can get a majority vote from their colleagues."[30] Nevertheless, the court ruled that a secondary-school teacher may be discharged for using in good faith a relevant teaching method regarded by experts of significant standing as serving a serious educational purpose, if he does not prove that it has the support of the preponderant opinion of the teaching profession or of the part of it to which he belongs. In such a case, the court held, the teacher merely must be given prior notice that the method is impermissible.

In reaching this conclusion, the court drew a distinction between teachers at the college or university level and teachers at the secondary level. The court said:

> The secondary school more clearly than the college or university acts *in loco parentis* with respect to minors. It is closely governed by a school board selected by a local community. The faculty does not have the independent traditions, the broad discretion as to teaching methods, nor usually the intellectual qualifications, of university professors. Among secondary school teachers there are often many persons with little experience. Some teachers and most students have limited intellectual and emotional maturity. Most parents, students, school boards, and members of the community usually expect the secondary school to concentrate on transmitting basic information, teaching "the best that is known and thought in the world," training by established techniques, and, to some extent at least, indoctrinating in the *mores* of the surrounding society. While secondary schools are not rigid disciplinary institutions, neither are they open forums in which mature adults, already habituated to social restraints, exchange ideas on a level of parity.[31]

The court also refused to accept the premise that the student at the secondary level is voluntarily in the classroom and "willing to be exposed to a teaching method which, though reasonable, is not approved by the school authorities or by the weight of professional opinion. A secondary-school student, unlike most college students, is usually required to attend school classes, and may have no choice as to his teacher."[32]

The court distinguished the cases involving the *Atlantic Monthly* article and the Vonnegut short story as cases where the court, from its own evaluation of the teaching method used, could conclude that use of the method was "plainly permissible . . . at least in the absence of an express proscription."[33] Because of "the risk of abuse involved in the technique of questioning students," the court determined, it could not conclude that the method used in the case at bar was "plainly permissible." However, since the teacher had not been given prior notice that his teaching method was impermissible, he was reinstated with back pay.

On appeal, the court of appeals rejected the trial court's formulation for weighing the circumstances in which a teacher's classroom speech or writing is constitutionally protected, suggesting that the formulation "would introduce more problems than it would resolve . . . [W]e see no substitute for a case-by-case inquiry into whether the legitimate interests of the authorities are demonstrably sufficient to circumscribe a teacher's speech."[34] Confessing that it was "not of one mind as to whether plaintiff's conduct fell within the protection of the First Amendment," the court found it unnecessary to resolve that issue since it agreed with the lower court that the teacher was denied due process because of the lack of warning.[35]

(3.) Have the courts generally considered the age of the students in determining whether a teacher's classroom discussion or assignment is protected?

Yes. As the court of appeals indicated in the "taboo-word" case, a court will look to see whether the discussion or assignment was appropriate for the age level of the students involved. In the case involving the Vonnegut short story, for example, the court noted that the school officials had failed to show that the assignment was "inappropriate reading for high school juniors. . . ."[36] In the case involving the *Atlantic Monthly* article, the court, posing the question whether "the shock was too great for high-school seniors to stand," expressed confidence that they were not "devoid of all discrimination or resistance."[37]

(4.) To what extent do the reactions of students or parents affect the teacher's constitutional right?

That some students or parents may be offended is not controlling. In the short-story case the teacher's assignment was held protected even though three of her students had asked to be excused and "several disgruntled parents" had called to complain.[38] The court implied that it might have reached a different result had the defendants shown a "significant disruption" of the processes of the school.[39] In the *Atlantic Monthly* case, the court, while not questioning "the good faith of the defendants in believing that some parents . . . [had] been offended," held that "their sensibilities are not the full measure of what is proper education."[40]

(5.) Do social-studies teachers have any constitutional protection from retaliation by school authorities for controversial discussion in the classroom?

Yes. In a recent case a high-school civics teacher was dismissed for "insubordination" following parental complaints about his discussion of controversial social and political issues, and his use of controversial materials, in the classroom. Among the matters which aroused parental ire were his truthful statement, in response to a student's classroom question, that he was not opposed to interracial marriages, and his teaching of a six-day unit on race relations. Some parents criticized his teaching of this unit, objecting to certain statements he made regarding race and prejudice and also to a true-false and multiple-choice test he administered to the students. One parent claimed that the written materials he assigned during the unit were propagandistic and imparted to a captive audience without giving students the opportunity to express opposing viewpoints.

The court held that the board's action was arbitrary and a denial of the teacher's rights under the First and Fourteenth Amendments, including his free-speech rights.[41] It noted that the teacher's two immediate supervisors generally had approved his teaching procedures and conduct; that the principal, who had reported the parental complaints to the board, had never visited the teacher's classroom and was wholly unfamiliar with his teaching methods; and that the board had acted without firsthand knowledge of what was transpiring in the classroom. Thus, there was only "minimal proof," apart from the teacher's own testimony, concerning the nature of his class discussions. The court concluded that "viewed overall, something approaching fair treatment of the various viewpoints on controversial issues was approached when all aspects of the course are considered." The court concluded that the teacher's classroom methods were "formulated and conducted within the ambit of accepted professional standards," and that his classroom statements neither materially and substantially interfered with the requirements of appropriate discipline nor subjected students unfairly to indoctrination and influence.[42]

Although the court warned that it is the teacher's "duty to be exceptionally fair and objective in presenting his personally held opinions" and "to actively and persuasively present different views, in addition to open discussion," it ruled that: "The freedom of speech of a teacher and a citizen of the United States must not be so lightly regarded that he stands in jeopardy of dismissal for raising controversial issues in an eager but disciplined classroom."[43] The court declared:

A teacher's methods are not without limits. Teachers occupy a unique position of trust in our society, and they must handle such trust and the instruction of young people with great care. On the other hand, a teacher must not be manacled with rigid regulations, which preclude full adaptation of the course to the times in which we live. It would be ill-advised to presume that a teacher would be limited, in essence, to a single textbook in teaching a course today in civics and social studies.[44]

The court also noted the importance of giving teachers discretion with regard to teaching method. Finding the teacher's objectives to be "proper to stimulate critical thinking, to create an awareness of our present political and social community and to enliven the educational process"—"all desirable goals"[45]—the court observed:

> While the best method might have been to take care to present written materials to support each viewpoint in controversy, the various class discussions which this Court finds did occur adequately fulfill the need for expression of dissident views. While the best method of testing over a unit on race and prejudice might have been a test in essay form, the objective true and false and multiple choice tests given, in light of the written material, were adequate. A responsible teacher must have freedom to use the tools of his profession as he sees fit. If the teacher cannot be trusted to use them fairly, then the teacher should never have been engaged in the first place.[46]

Adopting the rule which courts had previously applied to English teachers accused of discussing or assigning obscene words or materials, the court held that the teacher had a substantive constitutional right "to choose a teaching method, which, in the court's view, on the basis of expert opinion, served a demonstrated educational purpose. . . ."[47]

(6.) Have the courts generally considered the relevance of a teacher's classroom utterances to the subject matter being taught?

Yes. Relevance is a significant factor.[48]

Thus, a court refused to hold that observations on Vietnam and anti-Semitism uttered by an air-force teacher of a basic English class for foreign officers were constitutionally protected. The lesson plan he was supposed to follow at the time in question called for language instruction on the subjects "At the Dentist" and "How to Test a Used Car." Noting that his observations on Vietnam and anti-Semitism "would appear to have, at best, minimal relevance to the immediate classroom objectives," the court implied that the result might have been different had he been teaching current events, political science, sociology, or international relations.[49] Another court doubted that a teacher "had a constitutional right to teach politics in a course in economics."[50]

One court has expressed a disposition to interpret liberally the requirement of relevance. Disparaging the argument that a junior-college English teacher cannot teach notions of campus freedom in literature courses, the court stated: "[It] would obliterate cherished ideas about the relationship of teacher-pupil and the teacher's role in character building were instruction so closely confined to the technicalities of a particular subject or academic discipline. With its inexorable logic and predictability there may even be a great moral lesson in 2x2 equal 4."[51]

(7.) Must a teacher be given clear guidelines showing what types of classroom discussion or assignments are prohibited?

Yes, unless the activity is one which the teacher clearly ought to have recognized as forbidden.

In 1967, the United States Supreme Court invalidated laws of New York which, as implemented, required removal of a teacher from the public-school system for "treasonable or seditious" utterances or acts and barred employment in the public-school system of any person who "by word of mouth or writing willfully or deliberately advocates, advises, or teaches the doctrine" of forceful overthrow of government.[52] The statutes required an annual review of every teacher to determine whether any utterance of his, inside the classroom or out, came within the reach of the laws.[53] In holding these provisions unconstitutionally vague, the Court said: "When one must guess what conduct or utterance may lose him his position, one necessarily will 'steer far wider of the unlawful zone.' . . . The danger of that chilling effect upon the exercise of vital First Amendment rights must be guarded against by sensitive tools which clearly inform teachers what is being proscribed."[54]

A teacher may be confronted not merely with *vague* standards but with the total *absence* of standards. Several decisions have held that in the particular circumstances of the case the due process clause of the Fourteenth Amendment barred punishment of a teacher for allegedly offensive classroom assignments or discussion without prior notice, through a regulation or otherwise, that such conduct was forbidden.[55] As one court said, this protection is afforded because in his teaching capacity he is engaged in the exercise of what may plausibly be considered "vital First Amendment rights," and should not be forced to guess what speech may cost him his job. The court also noted that if a teacher did not have the right to be warned before he was discharged, he might be excessively timid and steer away from reasonable methods with which it is in the public interest to experiment.[56]

The courts have left open the possibility, however, that a teacher may "be on notice of impropriety from the circumstances of a case without the necessity of a regulation."[57] One court has suggested that such notice might be inferred from an informal rule, an understanding among teachers at the school or teachers generally, a body of disciplinary precedents, or precise canons of ethics, and that warning would not be required if the teacher engaged in "unforeseeable outrageous conduct which all men of good will would, once their attention is called to it, immediately perceive to be forbidden."[58]

In the "taboo word" case, the defense relied on a statement in the Code of Ethics of the Education Profession that the teacher "recognizes the supreme importance of the pursuit of the truth, devotion to excellence and the nurture of democratic citizenship." Rejecting the defense theory that this constituted sufficient warning, the court of appeals said: "As notice to the plaintiff that he should not have engaged in the act in question, this standard, although laudable, is impermissibly vague."[59]

Vague standards, or the absence of standards, may also

be subject to challenge on the ground that they vest excessive discretion in school authorities to approve of one form of speech and disapprove of another on the basis of personal whim. This vice is not cured by prior warning alone, but only by a clear *policy* or regulation. Arguably, school systems must adopt such a policy or regulation before a teacher can be punished for classroom speech in disregard of a prior warning.[60] The law on this point, however, is unsettled.

(8.) Does a teacher have a constitutional right to proselytize in the classroom?

It is doubtful that a teacher has such a right, at least at the elementary and perhaps at the secondary levels, where students may be particularly susceptible to the influence of their teachers. As the Supreme Court has said: "A teacher works in a sensitive area in a schoolroom. There he shapes the attitude of young minds towards the society in which they live. In this, the state has a vital concern."[61]

Thus, the courts have been "keenly aware of the state's vital interest in protecting the impressionable minds of its young people from *any* form of extreme propagandism in the classroom."[62] For example, a federal court upheld a decision not to renew the contract of a high-school social-studies teacher where there was substantial evidence that the teacher had abused his position by using his classroom "as his personal forum to promote union activities, to sanction polygamy, to attack marriage, to criticize other teachers and to sway and influence the minds of young people without a full and proper explanation of both sides of the issue."[63]

Another court held that "when reasonable alternatives for expression of dissent are available . . . a teacher is not constitutionally entitled to use the classroom as a forum for expression of disagreement with her administrators on internal affairs."[64]

Where such alternatives are unavailable, the court may reach a different result. One court, for example, upheld the constitutional right of a teacher to encourage her students to draw pictures, including pictures of wilted flowers, depicting how the students felt about the failure of the school administration to fix a broken water fountain in the classroom. The court also ruled that the teacher had a constitutional right, in the course of an authorized class on nutrition, to join in signing a student-initiated letter protesting the serving of cooked carrots rather than raw carrots in the school cafeteria.[65]

Of course, the Constitution does not shield from discipline a teacher who uses his classroom for partisan political purposes. As a California court once observed, ". . . advocacy before the scholars of a public school by a teacher of the election of a particular candidate for a public office . . . introduces into the school questions wholly foreign to its purposes and objects. . . ."[66] It seems apparent from these cases that the more questionable the relevance of a teacher's discussion to the subject matter of his course, the easier it will be for a court to find that he has unacceptably intruded his personal views into the classroom.[67]

A teacher may have somewhat more leeway at the college level. In one case, a junior-college teacher advised his class that the county superintendent of schools could be a good superintendent "but he spends too much time . . . [here the teacher stepped over to the wall and simulated licking his tongue in an up-and-down manner] licking up the Board." The court upheld the teacher's termination based partly on this incident on the ground that the teacher's activities in the presence of his students "were disruptive, an impairment of the teaching process, and not an example of the responsible dissent which should be fostered in the classroom." The court said, however, that "it cannot be questioned that the defendant had a right as a teacher and a citizen to differ with, to dissent from, and to criticize the superintendent," ruling only that "the *means of expression* used puts him far outside the protection of the First Amendment," and implying that a more decorous mode of criticism, even though in the classroom, would have been protected.[68]

Even at the elementary and secondary levels, it can

reasonably be argued that a teacher has a constitutional right to express his personal view if relevant to the subject matter, provided he refrains from seeking to win student converts but fairly presents all sides of the issue.[69] Indeed, a teacher who avoids answering a student's direct question about the teacher's personal opinion may well forfeit the respect of his class. It is also conceivable that a teacher who is disciplined because he has propagandized for an unpopular view might successfully challenge such action on equal protection grounds if he could show that the school authorities permitted teachers to propagandize for *orthodox* views.[70]

(9.) Is a teacher constitutionally entitled to wear in the classroom a badge, button or other insignia identifying himself with a particular cause?

The one reported case dealing with this question suggests that the answer turns on the maturity of the students and whether the school system can prove that the wearing of such insignia created or threatened to create substantial disruption in the school; that the teacher attempted to proselytize his students, or that students were in fact indoctrinated.

The case involved the dismissal of a probationary eleventh grade English teacher for wearing in class a black armband as a symbolic protest against the Vietnam War, in violation of his principal's directive. Rejecting the teacher's contention that he could not be disciplined because he was exercising his right of free speech, the New York Commissioner of Education stated: "If the subject matter involves conflicting opinions, theories or schools of thought, the teacher must present a fair summary of the entire range of opinion so that the student may have complete access to all facets and phases of the subject. Petitioner in this case, in wearing the black armband in his classroom, was presenting only one point of view on an important public issue on which a wide range of deeply held opinion and conviction exists."[71]

After the Commissioner's decision, the teacher filed a suit

under the Civil Rights Act. The trial court dismissed the suit, but the dismissal was reversed by the United States Court of Appeals, which ruled that the teacher's conduct was constitutionally protected speech.

The court of appeals relied upon a decision of the Supreme Court upholding the constitutional right of students to engage in similar symbolic speech in the classroom absent evidence demonstrating facts "which might reasonably have led school authorities to forecast substantial disruption of or material interference with school activities . . .".[72] The court of appeals noted that no such facts had been presented in the case at bar.

Although the court recognized that a school system has a legitimate interest in protecting impressionable school children from indoctrination, it ruled that the regulatory policy must be "drawn as narrowly as possible to achieve the social interests that justify it," and cannot restrict protected speech to an extent "greater than is essential to the furtherance of" those interests.[73] Citing the relative maturity of the teacher's students (16 or 17 years old), the absence of any attempt to proselytize them, and the lack of any evidence "that any student believed the armband to be anything more than a benign symbolic expression of the teacher's personal views,"[74] the court stated: "Recently, this country enfranchised 18-year olds. It would be foolhardy to shield our children from political debate and issues until the eve of their first venture into the voting booth. Schools must play a central role in preparing their students to think and analyze and to recognize the demagogue. Under the circumstances present here, there was a greater danger that the school, by power of example, would appear to the students to be sanctioning the very 'pall of orthodoxy' condemned in *Keyishian,* which chokes freedom of dissent."[75]

Expressing concern that the school board's regulation against political activity in the classroom might "be no more than the fulcrum to censor only that expression with which it disagrees,"[76] the court cited the allegation in the complaint that another teacher, without incurring any disciplinary sanction, had prominently displayed on a bulletin board in his classroom the slogan "Peace with Honor." The court also warned that "[u]nder the guise of beneficent concern for the welfare of school children, school authorities, albeit unwittingly, might permit prejudices of the community to prevail."[77]

It is not clear how far the courts will go in permitting teachers to engage in symbolic expression in the classroom. A teacher, for example, might well act at his peril if, however "benign" his intent and however innocuous the effect, he elected to sport a swastika on his arm while lecturing his students in trigonometry.

(10.) Does a teacher have a constitutional right to refuse to obey a demand by school authorities to proselytize in the classroom?

Although the courts have not definitely resolved the question, there are decisions suggesting that a teacher has such a right.

Under one view of education, teachers at the elementary- and secondary-school levels are charged with the role of transmitting to their wards not only knowledge but also the values and philosophies which predominate in the community. This view is exemplified by cases upholding the wartime dismissals of teachers opposed to war, such as Quakers and conscientious objectors, on the ground that they would not or could not impart patriotic values to their charges.[78]

It is doubtful, however, whether school authorities today could constitutionally require a teacher to proselytize, or to foster patriotism by means which conflict with the teacher's own convictions, religious or otherwise. That at least some courts would give such practices close scrutiny is indicated by recent decisions (discussed in detail in a subsequent portion of this book) holding that a teacher has a constitutional right to refuse to salute the flag or to lead his class in or recite the pledge of allegiance.[79]

NOTES

1. *See* Metzger, "The Age of the University," in R. Hofstadter and W. Metzger, *The Development of Academic Freedom in the United States* 275, 386-87 (1955); *Developments in the Law, Academic Freedom,* 81 Harv. L.Rev. 1045, 1051-52 (1968).
2. *Keyishian* v. *Board of Regents,* 385 U.S. 589, 603 (1967).
3. *Ibid. See also United States* v. *Associated Press,* 52 F.Supp. 362, 372 (S.D. N.Y. 1943).
4. 354 U.S. 234 (1957).
5. 354 U.S. at 249-50.
6. 354 U.S. at 250.
7. *Albaum* v. *Carey,* 283 F.Supp. 3, 10-11 (E.D. N.Y. 1968).
8. *Meyer* v. *Nebraska,* 262 U.S. 390, 399-400 (1923).
9. *See* Van Alstyne, *The Constitutional Rights of Teachers and Professors,* 1970 Duke L.J. 841, 855; N. Dorsen, *The Rights of Americans* 554-57 (1971).
10. Press release of Bryan in Chicago, June 2, 1925, Bryan MSS, 1925 [quoted in H. Beale, *Are American Teachers Free?* 257 (1936)].
11. *Scopes* v. *State,* 154 Tenn. 105, 289 S.W. 363 (1927).
12. *Epperson* v. *Arkansas,* 393 U.S. 97 (1968).
13. *Id.* at 105.
14. *Id.* at 109.
15. *Id.* at 113.
16. *Id.* at 113-14.
17. *Id.* at 116.
18. *See, e.g., Keefe* v. *Geanakos,* 418 F.2d 359 (1st Cir. 1969); *Parducci* v. *Rutland,* 316 F.Supp. 352 (M.D. Ala. 1970); *Mailloux* v. *Kiley,* 323 F.Supp. 1387 (D. Mass. 1971), *aff'd,* 448 F.2d 1242 (1st Cir. 1971).
19. *Parker* v. *Board of Educ.,* 237 F.Supp. 222 (D. Md. 1965), *aff'd,* 348 F.2d 464 (4th Cir. 1965), *cert. denied,* 382 U.S. 1030 (1966).
20. *Keefe* v. *Geanakos,* 418 F.2d 359 (1st Cir. 1969).
21. *Id.* at 361.
22. *Ibid.*
23. *Id.* at 362.
24. *Parducci* v. *Rutland,* 316 F.Supp. 352 (M.D. Ala. 1970).
25. *Id.* at 353-54.
26. *Id.* at 355-56.

27. *Id.* at 356.
28. *Ibid.*
29. *Mailloux* v. *Kiley*, 448 F.2d 1242, 1243 (1st Cir. 1971).
30. *Mailloux* v. *Kiley*, 323 F.Supp. 1387, 1391 (D. Mass. 1971), *aff'd*, 448 F.2d 1242 (1st Cir. 1971).
31. *Id.* at 1392.
32. *Ibid.*
33. *Id.* at 1390.
34. *Mailloux* v. *Kiley*, 448 F.2d 1242, 1243 (1st Cir. 1971).
35. *Ibid.*
36. *Parducci* v. *Rutland*, 316 F.Supp. 352, 356 (M.D. Ala. 1970).
37. *Keefe* v. *Geanakos*, 418 F.2d 359, 362 (1st Cir. 1969). *See also Mailloux* v. *Kiley*, 436 F.2d 565, 566 (1st Cir. 1971) ("[A]ge and sophistication of students" are pertinent factors); *Mailloux* v. *Kiley*, 323 F.Supp. 1387, 1389 (D. Mass. 1971); *Webb* v. *Lake Mills Community School District*, Civil No. 71-C-2053-C (N.D. Iowa May 26, 1972). *Compare Thompson* v. *Madison County Board of Educ.*, Civil No. 4692 (S.D. Miss. Mar. 8, 1972).
38. *Parducci* v. *Rutland*, 316 F.Supp. 352, 354 (M.D. Ala. 1970).
39. *Id.* at 356.
40. *Keefe* v. *Geanakos*, 418 F.2d 359, 361-62 (1st Cir. 1969).
41. *Sterzing* v. *Ft. Bend Independent School District*, Civil No. 69-H-319 (S.D. Tex. May 5, 1972).
42. *Ibid.*
43. *Id.* at 13-14.
44. *Id.* at 12-13.
45. *Id.* at 16.
46. *Id.* at 15-16.
47. *Id.* at 17. Compare *Springston* v. *King*, 340 F.Supp. 314, 316 (W.D. Va. 1972) (guidance counselor's claim that his reassignment was motivated by displeasure of school officials at his policy of confidentiality does not support a claim of denial of free speech).
48. *Mailloux* v. *Kiley*, 436 F.2d 565, 566 (1st Cir. 1970); *Mailloux* v. *Kiley*, 448 F.2d 1242, 1243 (1st Cir. 1971).
49. *Goldwasser* v. *Brown*, 417 F.2d 1169, 1177 (D.C. Cir. 1969), *cert. denied*, 397 U.S. 922 (1970).
50. *Ahern* v. *Board of Educ.*, 327 F.Supp. 1391, 1397 (D. Neb. 1971), *aff'd*, 456 F.2d 399 (8th Cir. 1972). *See also Thompson* v. *Madison County Board of Educ.*, Civil Action No. 4692 (S.D. Miss. Mar. 8, 1972).

51. *Pred* v. *Board of Public Instruction,* 415 F.2d 851, 857 n. 17 (5th Cir. 1969).

52. *Keyishian* v. *Board of Regents,* 385 U.S. 589 (1967).

53. *Id.* at 601-02.

54. *Id.* at 604. See also *Webb* v. *Lake Mills Community School District,* Civil No. 71-C-2053-C (N.D. Iowa May 26, 1972) p. 16 (invalidating, on this ground, the removal of a teacher from her position as drama coach because she had produced a play depicting drinking and using words "darn" and "son of a gun").

55. *Keefe* v. *Geanakos,* 418 F.2d 359, 362 (1st Cir. 1969); *Parducci* v. *Rutland,* 316 F.Supp. 352, 356-58 (M.D. Ala. 1970); *Mailloux* v. *Kiley,* 323 F.Supp. 1387 (D. Mass. 1971), aff'd, 448 F.2d 1242 (1st Cir. 1971); *Webb* v. *Lake Mills Community School District,* Civil No. 71-C-2053-C (N.D. Iowa May 26, 1972) p. 20; *Sterzing* v. *Ft. Bend Independent School District,* Civil No. 69-H-319 (S.D. Tex. May 5, 1972) p. 17 (teacher has right not to be discharged for use of a teaching method which was not proscribed by a regulation or "definitive" administrative action).

56. *Mailloux* v. *Kiley,* 323 F.Supp. 1387, 1392 (D. Mass. 1971). See also *Webb* v. *Lake Mills Community School District,* Civil No. 71-C-2053-C (N.D. Iowa May 26, 1972) p. 20.

57. *Keefe* v. *Geanakos,* 418 F.2d 359, 362 (1st Cir. 1969). See also *Mailloux* v. *Kiley,* 436 F.2d 565, 566 (1st Cir. 1971); *Parducci* v. *Rutland,* 316 F.Supp. 352, 357 (M.D. Ala. 1970).

58. *Mailloux* v. *Kiley,* 323 F.Supp. 1387, 1392-93 (D. Mass. 1971).

59. *Mailloux* v. *Kiley,* 448 F.2d 1242, 1243 (1st Cir. 1971).

60. *Cf. In re City and County of San Francisco,* 55 Lab. Arb. 970, 975 (1970).

61. *Shelton* v. *Tucker,* 364 U.S. 479, 485 (1960), quoting *Adler* v. *Board of Educ.,* 342 U.S. 485, 493 (1952).

62. *Parducci* v. *Rutland,* 316 F.Supp. 352, 355 (M.D. Ala. 1970). See also *Sterzing* v. *Ft. Bend Independent School District,* Civil No. 69-H-319 (S.D. Tex. May 5, 1972) pp. 12, 14; Van Alstyne, *The Constitutional Rights of Teachers and Professors,* 1970 Duke L.J. 841, 856.

63. *Knarr* v. *Board of School Trustees,* 317 F.Supp. 832, 836 (N.D. Ind. 1970), aff'd, 452 F.2d 649 (7th Cir. 1971).

64. *Ahern* v. *Board of Educ.,* 327 F.Supp. 1391, 1398 (D. Neb. 1971), aff'd, 456 F.2d 399 (8th Cir. 1972). See also *Robbins* v. *Board of Educ.,* 313 F.Supp. 642, 645, 647

(N.D. Ill. 1970) (teacher did not "necessarily" have a constitutional right to post on her classroom door a satirical memorandum regarding racially integrated Christmas decorations, especially in the context of a racially tense school climate).

65. *Downs* v. *Conway School District,* 328 F.Supp. 338, 339-41 (E.D. Ark. 1971).

66. *Goldsmith* v. *Board of Educ.,* 66 Cal. App. 157, 173, 225 Pac. 783, 789 (1924).

67. *See Goldwasser* v. *Brown,* 417 F.2d 1169 (D.C. Cir. 1969), *cert. denied,* 397 U.S. 922 (1970).

68. *Palo Verde Unified School District* v. *Hensey,* 88 Cal. Rptr. 570, 575, 9 Cal. App. 3d 967, 974 (1970).

69. *Sterzing* v. *Ft. Bend Independent School District,* Civil No. 69-H-319 (S.D. Tex. May 5, 1972) p. 14.

70. *Cf. James* v. *Board of Educ.,* No. 697 (2d Cir. May 24, 1972) p. 3253.

71. *In re Charles James,* No. 8195 (N.Y. Commissioner of Educ. Sept. 23, 1970).

72. *Tinker* v. *Des Moines Community School District,* 393 U.S. 503, 514 (1969).

73. *James* v. *Board of Educ.,* No. 697 (2d Cir. May 24, 1972) p. 3250.

74. *Id.* at 3251.

75. *Ibid.*

76. *Id.* at 3253.

77. *Ibid.*

78. *McDowell* v. *Board of Educ.,* 104 Misc. 564, 172 N.Y.S. 590 (1918); *State* ex rel. *Schweitzer* v. *Turner,* 155 Fla. 270, 19 So. 2d 832 (1944).

79. *Hanover* v. *Northrup,* 325 F.Supp. 170 (D. Conn. 1970); *State* v. *Lundquist,* 262 Md. 534, 278 A.2d 263 (1971); *Superintendent of Schools* v. *Jacobs,* Report of Bethuel L. Webster as Trial Examiner (1968) p. 11, cited favorably in *Frain* v. *Baron,* 301 F.Supp. 27, 32 (E.D. N.Y. 1969). *See also West Virginia State Board of Educ.* v. *Barnette,* 319 U.S. 624 (1943).

III. Freedom of Speech and Association Outside the Classroom

The American notion of academic freedom departs from the German concept in its concern for the teacher's "extra-mural" freedom. The German theory protected the teachers only in the classroom. Outside the university walls, teachers, like other citizens, were subject to repressive conditions. In the United States, with its traditions of free speech and expression, the teacher demanded the prerogative of free speech that was the birthright of other citizens. As an intellectual leader, moreover, the scholar may have special contributions to make in debate over public issues. Thus, the American idea of academic freedom has been enlarged to include the right of the teacher to express himself freely in his private capacity without reprisals by school or government authorities.[1]

Influenced in part by such philosophical and practical considerations, the courts increasingly have applied the Constitution to forbid legislative and administrative encroachments on the freedom of public-school teachers to advocate ideas, join causes, and engage in political activity outside the classroom.

UTTERANCES OUTSIDE THE CLASSROOM

In 1941 Howard Beale wrote: "In theory . . . [a teacher] is freer to advocate unpopular causes outside class than inside, but in practice the advocacy of unpopular causes in the community gets him into trouble more quickly than doing so in school."[2]

In one dramatic example, the entire faculty of Berea School was driven out in 1859 for abolitionism.[3] A similar fate may befall an educator in certain areas of the South today who takes too seriously his obligation to integrate the schools or who openly advocates or practices social equality between the races.

Surveys have shown that historically teachers have been afraid to take the unpopular side of economic questions, to attack local corruption, or even to criticize the President.[4] A report in 1941 declared: "Many [teachers] are afraid to advocate total disarmament or to criticize the Supreme Court for its refusal to admit pacifists to citizenship. Still more dare not declare that our entry into the World War was a mistake or praise war-time conscientious objectors. . . ."[5]

In time of war hysteria, teachers who express pacifist views or question the wisdom of the nation's course are fortunate to escape reprisals. Even today there are allegations of official retaliation against teachers who have publicly expressed opposition to the Vietnam conflict in communities where the prevailing sentiment supports the war.

School officials may be especially sensitive about speech by teachers critical of administration policies. The teacher's right to criticize may be resisted by such officials on the articulated ground that a teacher owes a duty of "loyalty" to his superiors.

(1.) Is a teacher subject to termination or discipline for out-of-class speech critical of school officials?

No categorical answer can be given. Although the Supreme Court has recognized that such criticism may be constitutionally protected, it has also warned that this protection may not exist where the criticism would seriously undermine close employment relationships or other conditions necessary to the effective operation of the school system.

The leading case is *Pickering* v. *Board of Education,*[6]

where a school board dismissed a teacher who wrote a letter to a newspaper editor which (1) attacked the board's handling of proposals to raise new school revenues and its allocation of resources between educational and athletic programs; and (2) charged the district superintendent with attempting to prevent teachers from criticizing a proposed bond issue. Although the letter was factually incorrect in several respects, the United States Supreme Court held that Pickering's dismissal violated his First Amendment right of free speech.

The Court first "unequivocally" rejected any suggestion that "even comments on matters of public concern that are *substantially correct* . . . may furnish grounds for dismissal if they are sufficiently critical in tone . . .",[7] at least where "[t]he statements are in no way directed towards any person with whom . . . [the teacher] would normally be in contact in the course of his daily work . . ."[8] and where "no question of maintaining either discipline by immediate superiors or harmony among coworkers is presented. . . ."[9] The Court hedged its ruling further in a footnote:

It is possible to conceive of some positions in public employment in which the need for confidentiality is so great that even completely correct public statements might furnish a permissible ground for dismissal. Likewise, positions in public employment in which the relationship between superior and subordinate is of such a personal and intimate nature that certain forms of public criticism of the superior by the subordinate would seriously undermine the effectiveness of the working relationship between them can also be imagined.[10]

The Court intimated "no views" as to how it would resolve any such cases, but concluded that Pickering's "employment relationships with the Board and, to a somewhat lesser extent, with the superintendent are not the kind of close working relationships for which it can persuasively be claimed that personal loyalty and confidence are necessary for their proper functioning."[11]

As for the false statements, the defendants had not shown such statements to have impeded the teacher's proper performance of his daily classroom duties or the regular operation of the schools. The Court ruled such interference will not be presumed, and in such circumstances "absent proof of false statements *knowingly or recklessly* made by him, a teacher's exercise of his right to speak on issues of public importance may not furnish the basis for his dismissal from public employment."[12] The Court stressed that:

[T]he question whether a school system requires additional funds is a matter of legitimate public concern on which the judgment of the school administration, including the School Board, cannot, in a society that leaves such questions to popular vote, be taken as conclusive. On such a question free and open debate is vital to informed decision-making by the electorate. Teachers are, as a class, the members of a community most likely to have informed and definite opinions as to how funds allotted to the operation of the schools should be spent. Accordingly, it is essential that they be able to speak out freely on such questions without fear of retaliatory dismissal."[13]

Pickering involved the dismissal of a teacher during his contract term. Subsequently, relying on *Pickering,* a federal court ordered reinstated three nontenured school community workers in Richmond, California, who had been denied re-employment in retaliation for their action in signing a petition urging defeat of a limited tax increase, sought by the school board, because the board members had "not addressed itself to the needs of the black community in their campaign."[14]

Similarly, a Utah federal court held unconstitutional actions of junior-college officials in denying a teacher permanent status and further employment in order to punish him for (1) supporting a particular candidate in a state political election; (2) opposing the college administration in his capacity as president and member of the executive committee of the faculty association; and (3) criticizing some administration policies during association meetings. Holding the actions of the defendants arbitrary and in violation of the Fourteenth Amendment, the court noted that one of the effects of such actions was to discourage free expression and free association by other members of the faculty.[15] The court found that the college president and the dean of academic affairs had made untrue, defamatory, and malicious statements to faculty members suggesting that the denial of permanent status and further employment was attributable to serious misconduct by the plaintiff. Finding that the actions of these and other defendants had damaged his reputation and rendered him unable to continue in his chosen profession, the court awarded him general damages of forty thousand dollars in addition to damages for loss of salary, as well as punitive damages of twenty-five hundred dollars each against the president and the dean respectively.[16]

Other cases involving application of the *Pickering* rule are discussed in the answers to subsequent questions in this chapter.

(2.) When does an issue become one of "public importance" so as to bring a teacher's speech within the Pickering **rule?**

The answer is not yet clear. One court held that a letter by an employee of a model-cities agency to its director severely criticizing the agency's hiring and promotion practices and complaining of salary preferences and unfair treatment, copies of which were sent to the mayor, one city commissioner and two agency department heads, was not protected under *Pickering*. The court relied in part on its conclusion that the letter "was not written in support of some public issue and was not published by the news media."[17] This decision, however, seems inconsistent with other decisions holding constitutionally protected a letter from a naval shipyard worker to the secretary of the navy criticizing favoritism in promotions[18] and a letter from a teacher to his school board critical of the board's failure to renew the contract of a probationary teacher.[19] The decision also conflicts with cases, previously discussed, extending qualified First Amendment protection to the day-to-day classroom activities of teachers.

(3.) Is a teacher's public criticism of his principal on a matter of public concern constitutionally protected?

Pickering does not clearly answer this question. In one portion of its opinion, the Court noted that Pickering's statements were "in no way directed towards any person with whom . . . [Pickering] would normally be in contact during his daily work as a teacher. Thus no question of maintaining either discipline by immediate superiors or harmony among co-workers is presented here."[20] In another part of its opinion, the Court seemed more narrowly concerned with distinguishing situations involving "close working relationships" demanding "personal loyalty and confidence"[21] and superior-subordinate relationships of a "personal and intimate" nature which would be impaired by public criticism.[22]

In one case, a state court held that statements of teachers attacking the school superintendent were not protected under *Pickering* where, among other things, there were only two schools and thirty teachers in the entire system, and the superintendent dealt directly with all the teachers and "was in fact the . . . principal as well."[23] The court ruled that the teachers' actions "were directed toward a person with whom . . . [they] would normally be in contact in the course of their daily work as teachers, and where a question of maintaining discipline by an immediate superior was involved."[24]

In an Indiana case, however, a federal court held that a teacher—president of his local teacher association and a member of the negotiating team—had a constitutional right under *Pickering* to state at a meeting of the teacher association that "the school administration was trying to

buy them off with small items at the expense of big ones."[25]
The teacher's comment was directed at least in part toward
the actions of his own principal, who had called the
teacher into his office, stated that the comment reflected
directly upon the principal, and unsuccessfully demanded
an apology. When the teacher refused to retract the statement at a later meeting with the superintendent and principal, he was denied re-employment. The court ordered the
school authorities to renew the teacher's contract.

Certainly the Court in *Pickering* could not have intended
to insulate even "immediate superiors" from all criticism
by teachers. If, for example, a teacher has knowledge that
his department head is embezzling school funds, the teacher
has not only the privilege but the duty to report the matter
to the proper authorities. Similarly, if a teacher feels that
his immediate superior is wrong on a matter not adequately
covered by a grievance procedure, the teacher may well
have the right to petition higher authorities in the system
for relief or voice his concerns to other teachers. In *Tinker*
v. *Des Moines Community School District*,[26] the Supreme
Court, speaking to a somewhat different but related issue
involving the exercise of First Amendment rights in the
school context, said that "[i]n order for . . . school officials
to justify prohibition of a particular expression of opinion,
. . . [they] must be able to show that . . . [their] action
was caused by something more than a mere desire to avoid
the discomfort and unpleasantness that always accompany
an unpopular viewpoint."[27] In *Tinker,* the Court formulated the rule that First Amendment rights in the context
of a school may be curtailed only when their exercise
threatens to "materially and substantially disrupt the work
and discipline of the school."[28] And the Court has made
it clear that the burden of proving with facts the existence
of such a threat is on the State.[29] These principles were
only recently reaffirmed by the Court.[30]

**(4.) Must a teacher's out-of-class statement be mild or
moderate in tone in order to receive constitutional protection?**

No. A teacher's constitutional protection is not lost because his comments "strongly challenge or cause severe criticism of . . . his nominal superior"; are framed "in language likely to be offensive," or are less discreet than professional ethics might have dictated.[31]

In a New Hampshire case, for example, a teacher who was an active and outspoken member of the teachers' negotiating committee issued a series of press releases accusing the school board of "high-handed treatment" and "utter disregard" of its employees. The releases irritated the superintendent, who felt that they created public animosity toward the board and constituted unprofessional conduct. Subsequently, after becoming chairman of the negotiating committee, the teacher severely criticized the school board at a teacher association meeting, and stated that he had no personal respect for the school board negotiating team, the school board itself, or the superintendent. The teacher's contract was not renewed. Concluding that the decision was motivated primarily by the press releases and the teacher's statements at the association meeting, the court held that the nonrenewal violated his constitutional rights of free speech and association, and directed that he be reinstated with back pay.[32]

In a similar case, a Delaware court awarded the same relief to a teacher who had been dismissed for writing and distributing to other teachers in the district a newsletter accusing the board's negotiators of bad-faith bargaining with the teachers' association. The letter falsely accused the board's negotiators of committing an "utter and complete fabrication" in categorically denying the existence of funds with which to meet the teachers' salary requests. Believing, erroneously, in the availability of $115,000, the teacher asserted that the board "could give the teachers everything they asked for and still buy a lot more books and supplies for the children." Holding this to be protected speech, the court observed that the newsletter had a limited distribution, that oral retractions had been made by the association at teacher meetings in every school in the district, that there was no substantial evidence of any connection between the newsletter and the subsequent defeat of a school district referendum, and that the teacher's statements, though false, had not been recklessly made. Relying on *Pickering,* the court stated: "It is equally important where a school board and a teachers' association are negotiating over funds available for a contract that a teacher be able to speak out freely to members of the Association without fear of retaliatory dismissal by the school board."[33]

In a New York case a high-school teacher was suspended without pay for distributing to his fellow teachers copies of a letter he had written to his school board critical of the board's failure to renew the contract of a probationary teacher. In addition to factual inaccuracies, the letter contained "strident" comments. The court noted that there was no proof that the inaccuracies were the result of reckless or intentional falsehood, or that the teacher's indiscretions had any harmful effects within the school system. Partly in light of *Pickering,* the court held: "Indiscreet bombast in an argumentative letter, to the limited extent present here, is insufficient to sanction disciplinary action. Otherwise, those who criticize in any area where criticism is permissible would either be discouraged from exercising their right or would be required to do so in such innocuous terms as would make the criticism seem ineffective or obsequious."[34]

Another court, however, held that a teacher who stooped to name-calling and personal invective was not sheltered by the Constitution from the consequences of his acts. The court ruled that a probationary teacher's statements at a public school board hearing calling his administrative supervisor a liar and challenging the integrity of the board's entire administrative staff were not constitutionally protected and that the board's refusal to renew his contract because of such statements did not violate his right to free speech.[35]

It is not clear at what point "strident" comment becomes personal invective and loses its constitutional protection.

(5.) Are there circumstances in which a teacher is constitutionally entitled to use profanity in publicly criticizing his school system?

Yes. In a Texas case a state university rescinded an offer of re-employment as a teaching assistant which it had extended to the plaintiff because, at a "rock" concert held on the campus, she had strongly criticized the university administration and its policies, cited the university as a prime oppressor of human beings, and stated that the "system" as represented at the local level at the university "fucks over" students. The evidence showed that to the younger generation the compound verb "fuck over" means "oppress." Noting the lack of any showing that teachers who publicly use profanity are likely to be inferior teachers, that use of profanity in front of students is likely to cause the students to disrespect the teacher, or that use of profanity outside the classroom indicates bad moral character or inability to perform the teaching function competently, the court held the speech constitutionally protected and ordered the plaintiff reinstated, stating:

> The University has approached this matter as if plaintiff, by the mere incantation of the words "fucks over," could taint her listeners and the University in some manner, thereby justifying exorcism of this idiom and its user from the environs of the University . . . That the use of one word in lieu of another may conform more closely to the canons of good taste does does not justify severe sanctions against those who use the offending word. To prohibit particular words substantially increases the risk that ideas will also be suppressed in the process.[36]

Whether, and in what circumstances, similar speech uttered outside the classroom by a high-school or elementary-school teacher would be protected is unclear.

(6.) Is a teacher free to discuss problems in his school system on radio or television?

Yes, subject to the qualifications set forth in *Pickering*. For example, one court held that a police officer's statements on public television that the reporting system and patrol procedure in the police department were problems, that department morale had "hit its lowest ebb," and that he felt "the bottom would fall out of [the] . . . City" within the next six months if the situation continued, were permissible free speech for which the officer could not be disciplined. The court noted that the statements were not directed toward a superior with whom he would come into frequent contact and were not shown to have affected discipline or harmony or the effectiveness of the department.[37] A teacher would appear to have constitutional protection at least equivalent to that of an employee of a para-military organization.

(7.) Does a teacher have the right to complain publicly about the operation of his school system even if a grievance procedure exists for processing such complaints?

Probably not. In *Pickering*, the United States Supreme Court left the door open to "narrowly drawn grievance procedures" which would require employees "to submit complaints about the operation of the schools to their superiors for action thereon prior to bringing the complaints before the public."[38]

The grievance procedure, however, must be adequate to deal with the particular complaint. In one case, city welfare investigators complained in a letter to an HEW official of the workload in the city welfare department and also declared that the state, by not reducing the workload, failed to qualify for federal contributions. The court ruled that the letter raised issues "not personal to them" but involved "general policies and practices in carrying out the Department's function."[39] Therefore, the court held, the investigators were not required to exhaust a grievance procedure dealing with the *individual* problems of employees and not designed "to deal with such broad issues as those raised in the . . . letter."[40]

(8.) Is a teacher constitutionally protected from discharge or discipline for bringing injustices or problems in his school system to the attention of his superiors or other employees in the system?

Yes, although the teacher may have to exhaust a "narrowly drawn grievance procedure" adequate to deal with the complaint.[41]

Thus, a Mississippi federal district court held protected under *Pickering* the action of a black teacher who mailed documents protesting alleged racial discrimination against black teachers in her school system to the superintendent, as well as other public officials.[42]

In addition to possessing certain free speech rights as elaborated in *Pickering,* a teacher has the right to petition his government for redress of grievances—a classic form of freedom of expression entitled to "the utmost protection of the Constitution."[43] He cannot be forced to surrender this right, any more than his right of free speech, as a condition of public employment.

For example, a school policy in Arkansas stated: "No petition for any purpose may be circulated in any building without the approval of the Superintendent of Schools." The superintendent concluded that a teacher violated the policy because of the following incidents:

(1) In her second-grade class, the authorized text and materials discussed the relative nutritional values of many foods and stated that the nutritional properties of raw carrots exceeded those of cooked carrots. The teacher permitted a student to prepare a letter, which was sent to the cafeteria supervisor, requesting that raw carrots be served instead of cooked carrots. The letter—which the court found to embody a teaching technique suggested by the school system itself—was signed by the teacher as well as the students.

(2) At a time when a water fountain in her room was broken and the temporary water supply—consisting of a plastic bucket and cups provided by the teacher at her own expense for her pupils—was exhausted and

an art class was beginning, the teacher asked the pupils to draw pictures of their neighbors in the classroom and express in the rough drawings the way that each one of the children in the class felt. Some pupils drew pictures of children lying down asking for water and pictures of wilted flowers. The teacher exhibited some of these drawings to the principal.

(3) The teacher sent personal notes to other teachers asking them whether they found effusions from an open incinerator on the school playground, which presented a danger to the health and safety of the children and teachers, objectionable.

The court held that the refusal to renew the contract of the teacher—who had taught in the Arkansas public schools for more than twenty-five years and for several years in the school system—on the basis of these alleged violations of the school policy was arbitrary and unreasonable and in violation of her First and Fourteenth Amendment rights of free speech and freedom peaceably to petition for redress of grievances.[44]

(9.) Is a teacher constitutionally protected in going over the heads of his superiors to bring injustices or problems in his school system to the attention of higher authorities outside the system?

Yes, although here again, the teacher may have to exhaust any adequate "narrowly drawn grievance procedure."[45]

In one case decided after *Pickering*, a probationary teacher in the job corps claimed he was fired for writing a letter to an OEO inspector who had inspected the job-corps center and invited the teacher's communication. The letter asked the OEO to look into the teacher's reversion from acting principal teacher to ordinary teaching, suggested that the center "should get rid of its Director and other officials to make it run like it should," and asserted that too many people in high positions had come from the other side of the tracks and had no understanding of the problems the "black boys have had to face."[46] The United States Court of Claims held that if, as alleged, the teacher had been fired as a result of his letter, his First Amendment right to petition for redress of grievances would have been infringed, and a trial was necessary to resolve the question of motive.

Earlier, the same court had ruled that the discharge of a naval shipyard worker for writing the secretary of the navy a letter charging superior officials with favoritism in promotions was an unconstitutional infringement of the right of the worker to petition for redress of grievances. Anticipating the *Pickering* rule, the court held that the defamatory statements were not shown to have been wilfully false or made with reckless disregard for the truth. The court pointed out the importance of keeping open the channels through which employees can call alleged derelictions or injustices to the attention of their superiors.[47]

In another case, a state court ruled that a letter by city welfare-department investigators to the director of the bureau of family services in HEW complaining of the workload in their department could not furnish a basis for discipline, in light of *Pickering*, where there was no showing that the investigators neglected their duties or that the letter interfered with the city's welfare program or created discipline problems or disharmony among fellow employees.[48]

(10.) Do the rights of free speech and petition protect a teacher who complains to his congressman, state legislator, or other elected representative about alleged injustices in his school system?

Yes, again subject to the possible requirement that the teacher exhaust any "narrowly drawn grievance procedure" designed to deal with the particular complaint.[49] Similar protection would appear to extend to a teacher who encourages another teacher to file such a complaint.[50]

The complaining teacher, however, must be careful to avoid conveying the impression that he speaks for the school board. Where a teacher wrote a letter to a state legislator complaining of alleged under-financing of the program for handicapped children in which she worked, and represented that she expressed the views of the school board, the court refused to hold the letter constitutionally protected. Concluding that she "had the right to write a letter to her Representative and otherwise express her opinions as a citizen," the court held that the teacher "had no right . . . to speak for the Board or to misrepresent its position."[51]

(11.) Are a teacher's out-of-class statements on controversial political or social issues which do not involve criticism of school authorities constitutionally protected?

Yes. A teacher would appear to have greater freedom to speak out on issues of this kind, since considerations of confidentiality clearly are not involved, and whatever disharmony in working relationships such speech might cause would be solely a function of the disagreement inherent in conflicting views.

In one case, a court held unconstitutional the expulsion of a peace-corps volunteer on the faculty of the University of Concepción in Chile for publishing a letter in a local Chilean newspaper, attacking the American involvement in Vietnam and peace-corps policy concerning the freedom of volunteers to criticize U.S. foreign policy. Even though the teacher was speaking in a foreign country, and arguably was compromising American foreign policy, the court said: "To permit a termination such as this would be to value bureaucratic paranoia over the central commitment of the First Amendment to 'uninhibited, robust, and wide-open debate on public issues.' "[52]

Similarly, a court refused to dismiss a complaint under the Civil Rights Act by a Mississippi teacher who alleged that his First Amendment rights were violated by the refusal of a state college to employ him because of his testimony for the defense in a criminal-obscenity trial.[53] Another court held that a valid claim under the Civil Rights Act was stated by a professor at a state college in Virginia who asserted that a recommended salary increase had been rescinded because he had written a letter to the editor of *Redbook* magazine praising the author of an article on premarital sex, identifying himself as a professor at the college, and indicating that he intended to use some of the author's comments in his teaching.[54]

In light of these cases, a 1940 decision of a New York state court revoking the appointment of Bertrand Russell as professor of philosophy in the City College of New York because his writings on sex and marriage demonstrated that he lacked "good moral character" is of dubious vitality today.[55]

(12.) Does a teacher's right of free speech extend to participation in a mass demonstration during his off-duty time?

Yes, but only to the extent that the demonstration is protected by the Constitution. For example, where the demonstration disrupts the normal functioning of the educational institution, the teacher will be on weak ground if he contends, in a disciplinary proceeding, that he was merely exercising his constitutional right to free speech.

In a recent case a professor at the University of Nebraska participated in a student occupation of a campus ROTC building to protest the military invasion of Cambodia and the killing and wounding of students at Kent State by the national guard. Because a number of demonstrators, not including the teacher, threatened violence and interference with a scheduled class, the university authorities canceled it. This was one of the factors relied upon by the Board of Regents in refusing to reappoint the professor. Upholding this ground for nonreappointment, the court said:

> It will not do for Professor Rozman to claim that neither he nor most of the others in the group would have interfered with the class. When one chooses to join a group which is largely leaderless and unstructured, he must assume, not only the benefits of the group, but the disabilities of the group, as well . . . When the group chooses not to communicate with a

united voice, it must bear the consequences of splintered voices.[56]

The court also sustained, as grounds for the university's refusal to reappoint the professor, his intrusion into the negotiations between the students and the administration and his action in remaining and linking arms with other demonstrators following directives from the university president—determined by the court to have been reasonable under the circumstances—to vacate the building. With respect to the latter activity, the court concluded that one fair interpretation of the professor's conduct was that he was defying the directives.[57]

(13.) Does a teacher's right to free speech include the right to take leave in order to participate in a mass demonstration?

It is questionable whether a teacher has an absolute right to take such leave. In one case. the University of North Carolina failed to renew the contract of a teacher who had canceled a class scheduled to be held on Vietnam Moratorium Day. The teacher was charged with violating a university policy subjecting to discharge any faculty member who, with intent to disrupt the normal operations of the university, wilfully failed to carry out his assigned duties. Rejecting the argument that the activities for which he was punished were political expressions protected by the First Amendment, the court declared:

Employment, in both the public and private sectors of society, makes certain demands upon the individual which are not made upon a person unemployed. . . . When the plaintiff accepted the position of instructor, he knew that there would be some hours of the week during which he was expected to be present and conduct a class. That the failure to carry out this responsibility was because he was elsewhere exercising his right of free expression does not excuse his unwillingness to perform those duties which he had undertaken. The protection of the First Amendment is not a shield behind which one may stand to avoid the consequences of a breach of a reasonable contract of employment.[58]

The court also refused to accept the teacher's contention that the policy violated the equal-protection clause of the Fourteenth Amendment because faculty members who absented themselves from class for political reasons and made provision to insure that the educational program did not suffer were penalized while those absent for personal or professional reasons who made similar arrangements were not disciplined. The court rejected this argument on the narrow ground that the policy subjected to discharge only those who refused to carry out assigned duties *with intent to obstruct* the normal operations of the university, and a majority of the university hearing committee which heard his case had found the requisite intent.[59]

A school system, of course, cannot deny a requested leave in order to deter protected speech.[60]

(14.) Does the Constitution afford protection to teachers in their out-of-class communications with other teachers on school property concerning matters of public importance?

Yes, although it is not clear how far such protection extends.

As the Supreme Court has stated, and the cases giving constitutional protection to classroom expression by teachers make clear, teachers do not "shed their constitutional rights to freedom of speech or expression at the schoolhouse gate."[61] The California Supreme Court, for example, ruled invalid, as a violation of the free-speech and petition guarantees of the First and Fourteenth Amendments, a school board regulation prohibiting teachers from circulating a petition on school premises during duty-free lunch periods. The petition in question was a controversial document addressed to the governor and state and local school officials opposing proposed cutbacks in funds for public education.[62] The court recognized that freedom of speech contemplates *effective* communication, and that school premises are the most effective place for teachers to communicate with each other.

Similarly, where a school policy prohibited the circulation of a petition in a school building without the superintendent's approval, and the superintendent interpreted the policy to bar a teacher from sending personal notes to other teachers asking them whether they found the effusions from an open incinerator on the school playground objectionable, the nonrenewal of the teacher in part for sending the notes was held to violate her First Amendment rights of free speech and petition.[63]

Teachers, however, should avoid utilizing time which is supposed to be devoted to school affairs in order to draft or discuss a letter or petition, and should refrain from conveying the impression that the petition represents school-system policy.[64]

(15.) Does a teacher forfeit his constitutional protection if his out-of-class communication on school property is so controversial as to pose a threat of conflict or disruption of the school system?

Not necessarily. The Supreme Court has said: "[I]n our system, undifferentiated fear or apprehension of disturbance is not enough to overcome the right to freedom of expression. Any departure from absolute regimentation may cause trouble. Any variation from the majority's opinion may inspire fear. Any word spoken, in class, in the lunchroom, or on the campus, that deviates from the views of another person may start an argument or cause a disturbance. But our Constitution says we must take this risk. . . ."[65]

In the California case discussed in the answer to the previous question, the court held that the fact that the controversial petition might foment discord and disturbance within the school system was not sufficient to justify the restriction imposed even though the teachers had been authorized to hold meetings on school property after school hours for the purpose of circulating the petition. Observing that "[t]olerance of the unrest intrinsic to the expression of controversial ideas is constitutionally required even in the schools,"[66] the court held that the board could not constitutionally limit circulation of the petition except to ward off a real and imminent danger which involved far more than "public inconvenience, annoyance or unrest."[67]

(16.) Do teachers have a constitutional right to communicate with other teachers through faculty mailboxes or school bulletin boards?

The cases are in conflict. In a Missouri case a teacher claimed she was not rehired because she had placed letters criticizing the Missouri State Teachers' Association convention in the personal mailboxes of other teachers at her school, and posted a congratulatory sign on the school bulletin board announcing that a previously demoted teacher had been transferred to a better position. The court held that the action of the board in not rehiring her did not violate her right of free speech, and that the plaintiff's actions had properly been regarded by the board as "insubordination."[68]

In contrast, a federal court in New York ruled that a school board regulation prohibiting, except for certain limited, specific items, distribution of all literature by teachers through faculty mailboxes, was overbroad and violated the First Amendment right of the teachers in the district. As did the court in the California case, the New York court quoted the admonition of the Supreme Court that teachers do not "shed their constitutional right to freedom of speech or expression at the schoolhouse gate."[69]

In the New York case, the court rejected the contention "that the Board, as vested owner of school premises, has the absolute right to direct how its facilities may be used. . . ."[70] The court concluded that any restriction upon the right of teachers to communicate with each other through faculty mailboxes must be based on facts which might reasonably lead school authorities to forecast substantial disruption of or material interference with school activities, and no such facts were presented. "The fact that 'tension and turmoil' surround the collective bargaining process," the court determined, "although undoubtedly true, is not the kind of interference that would save this wide prohibition."[71]

(17.) Can a faculty adviser to a student organization be dismissed or disciplined because the organization expresses controversial views or extends a speaking invitation to a controversial speaker?

No, at least where the activity of the organization is constitutionally protected. In one case, a student organization at an Arkansas state college sent a letter to an off-campus church questioning its policies on racial integration and extended a speaking invitation to a couple who had militant views and were seeking substantial changes in race relations. Because of the letter and the organization's refusal to withdraw the invitation, the college administrators imposed sanctions upon the organization, its officers, and its faculty advisers. The court held that the imposition of the sanctions violated the First Amendment rights of the faculty advisers as well as the students to free expression and association.[72]

Occasionally a school system may dismiss or discipline the faculty adviser to a student newspaper or magazine for failing to censor the publication. Although there is some conflict in the decisions, the courts have given increasing constitutional protection to student publications—particularly protections against prior restraint.[73] At least to the extent that the activity of the student publication is constitutionally protected, its faculty adviser would appear to share its immunity from sanctions.

CIVIL RIGHTS AND POLITICAL ACTIVITY

(1.) May a teacher be discharged or disciplined for engaging in peaceful civil rights activity during his off-duty time?

No. Such activity—at least to the extent that it is protected by the First and Fourteenth Amendments to the

Constitution as a form of speech, assembly, or petition—
cannot form the basis for discharge or discipline.

Although, broadly considered, civil rights activity may
involve "political" activity, "[t]here is virtually no justification for restricting the right of a teacher to engage in
nonpartisan advocacy of social or political reform absent a
showing that such activity reflects substantially on his performance in class. . . . Furthermore, petition for redress
of social grievances is the classic form of freedom of
expression and should carry with it the utmost protection of
the first amendment."[74]

In *Johnson* v. *Branch*,[75] the contract of a black nontenured teacher in a North Carolina town, who had been active
in civil rights demonstrations and voter registration and voting activity, was not renewed. The United States Court of
Appeals for the Fourth Circuit concluded that the reasons
assigned by the school board were so trivial as to (1)
render the nonrenewal arbitrary and capricious; and
(2) warrant the inference that the nonrenewal was actually
based on the teacher's civil rights activities. The court held
the nonrenewal unconstitutional on both grounds.

Other courts also have ruled unconstitutional as infringe-
ments upon freedom of political expression or association
the discharge or refusal to rehire nontenured teachers because of their participation in civil rights activities.[76] In
one case a black teacher in Mississippi, to express displeasure at the actions of the school board in terminating
her husband's employment and its alleged racially discriminatory policies, drew a picture depicting a black man
hanging on a cross with blood spilling from his side, in
addition to writing a poem and drafting a call for help. The
picture contained spiritual quotations and several questions.
One question, similar to the others, was "Were you there
when the black principals and teachers were fired?" Also
appearing on the picture was the statement, "One of these
days all mankind will have justice." These documents were
mailed to numerous persons, including the superintendent
and other local and national public officials. The teacher
was denied re-employment by the board, at least in part in

retaliation for her criticism reflected in the documents. The
court ordered her reinstated and held that she was entitled
to recover damages, ruling that her activities in regard to
the documents were constitutionally protected under *Pickering*.[77]

A teacher forfeits his constitutional protection if he
exceeds the legitimate bounds of criticism and protest
sheltered by the First Amendment. In a West Virginia case
a spokesman for black militants on a state-college campus
was rejected by a county school board as a student practice
teacher because he had threatened the life of the director
of student teachers, challenged the security officer to physical combat, and issued inflammatory bulletins inciting
others to violence on campus and the destruction of school
property. The court repudiated his claim that the board had
violated his free-speech rights.[78]

A public employee, moreover, has no constitutional right
to [subordinate] . . . public duties to . . . [his] personal
prepossessions,"[79] and civil rights activities are subject to
this rule.[80] A teacher who allows his personal feelings about
social injustice to impair his effectiveness as a teacher or
the effective operation of his school system should not
expect to receive constitutional protection for his actions.

(2.) May a teacher be dismissed or disciplined for taking an active part in politics during his off-duty time?

Only if the restriction is justified by a countervailing
state interest. It is not clear whether the state interest must
be merely *legitimate,* or whether it also must be *compelling.*

The courts have made it clear that the right to engage in
political expression and association is protected by the
First Amendment.[81] In a number of cases the courts have
dealt with the question whether, and to what extent, a
public employee may be compelled to relinquish these
rights as a condition of his public employment.

In 1947, in *United Public Workers* v. *Mitchell*,[82] the
United States Supreme Court, by a five-four vote, rejected
a constitutional challenge to provisions of the Hatch Act
prohibiting federal employees from taking an active part

in political management or political campaigning. Although the *Mitchell* decision has been followed by many lower federal courts,[83] it is questionable whether the Supreme Court would reach the same conclusion today.

The majority opinion in *Mitchell* elaborately deferred to the judgment of Congress concerning the supposed evils of partisan political activity by federal employees. Subsequent decisions of the Supreme Court—requiring a showing of a compelling governmental interest to justify an infringement upon basic liberties,[84] and rejecting the concept that public employment is a "privilege" subject to whatever conditions the government sees fit to impose[85]—suggest that the Court would give the Hatch Act much closer scrutiny today.

In reliance upon these later decisions, the Supreme Court of California in 1964 invalidated on First Amendment grounds a "little Hatch Act" prohibiting any county officer or employee in the classified civil service from, among other things, "taking part in political management or affairs in any political campaign or election . . . other than to cast his vote or to privately express his opinion." The court voided the statute on the ground that it was not supported by a compelling governmental interest and was broader "than . . . required to preserve the efficiency and integrity of" the public service.[86]

In a more recent case, a school board in Texas, relying upon its own regulation banning all political activity by teachers except voting, refused to re-employ a teacher at least in part because of his participation in political activities. Ruling for the teacher, the federal court held that "[t]he complete ban on the right of teachers to express political opinions and engage in political activity is inconsistent with the First Amendment guarantee of freedom of speech, press, assembly and petition."[87] The court observed that although the school board might "have a legitimate interest in protecting its educational and administrative activities from undue political activity . . . that is, activity which may materially and substantially interfere with the requirements of appropriate discipline in the operation of the school," the board could not pursue such purposes "by means that broadly stifle fundamental personal liberties when the ends sought can be more narrowly achieved."[88] The court expressed concern that such a regulation "muzzles some of the most influential citizens of smaller communities" and threatens popular government by depriving the community of the political participation and interest of these individuals.[89]

The trend reflected in these cases is continuing. In 1971, the United States Court of Appeals for the Fifth Circuit, in *Hobbs* v. *Thompson*,[90] held unconstitutional a city charter and ordinance prohibiting firemen from "contributing money to any candidate, soliciting votes, or prominently identifying themselves in a political race with or against any candidate for office." Noting that the regulatory scheme had been construed to forbid political bumper stickers, the court concluded that the scheme effectively rendered firemen "political eunuchs."[91] Observing that the Supreme Court's approach in *Mitchell* was "no longer good law,"[92] the court held that precision of regulation was required; that the scheme was fatally vague and overbroad,[93] and that since there was no intimation of a compelling state interest for the blackout of a fireman's bumper sticker, the resulting infringement upon political activity was unconstitutional.[94]

Subsequently, a federal district court in Rhode Island struck down a city charter provision prohibiting a member of the classified civil service from making "any contribution to the campaign funds of any political organization or candidate for public office or taking any part in the management of any political organization or in the conduct of any political campaign" other than to express his opinion and cast his vote.[95] The court, agreeing that the force of *Mitchell* had been vitiated, held that the provision was overbroad, vague and violated the First Amendment. The court said: "While it may be permissible to restrict political activities such as using official authority for partisan political purposes, political coercion of subordinates, or non-compliance with the merit system in promotion, the shotgun approach taken here is impermissible."[96]

In the Rhode Island case the court said:

> It has been estimated that by 1968 there were, excluding members of the armed forces, some three million federal employees and nine million State and local government employees, representing approximately 15 percent of the total working force. . . Restrictions on the freedom of political expression of such a large portion of the population is a matter of much concern.[97]

Other courts also have pointed to the burgeoning force of public employees and warned that our institutions of representative government are imperiled by "[r]estrictions on public employees which . . . advance no compelling public interest commensurate with the waiver of constitutional rights which they require"[98] or which are "not precisely confined to remedy specific evils."[99] Said one court: "As the number of persons employed by government . . . continues to grow the necessity of preserving for them the maximum practicable right to participate in the political life of the republic grows with it."[100]

(3.) May a teacher constitutionally be forced to resign his teaching position if he becomes a candidate for public office?

The decisions are in conflict. Several courts, however, relying upon Supreme Court rulings subsequent to the *Mitchell* case, have held that the government cannot constitutionally impose broad prohibitions forbidding a public employee from running for public office on pain of losing his job.

In 1966, the Supreme Court of Oregon struck down state statutes forbidding a civil-service employee from becoming a candidate for elective office unless he immediately resigned from his civil-service position. The plaintiff was a local deputy sheriff who announced his intention to become a candidate for sheriff, and sought a declaratory judgment

concerning his right to run for that office. The court held
that ". . . running for public office is one of the means of
political expression which is protected by the First Amendment. The right to engage in political activity is implicit in
the rights of association and free speech guaranteed by the
amendment."[101] Tracing the development of constitutional
law since the *Mitchell* decision, the court concluded that:

> [A] revolution has occurred in the law relative to the
> state's power to limit federal First Amendment rights.
> Thirty years ago, the statutes now under consideration
> would have been held to be constitutional. . . . This is
> no longer possible in view of the intervening decisions
> of the United States Supreme Court.[102]

The court, while indicating that there would have been a
compelling state interest warranting a *narrowly drawn*
statute preventing a public employee from *running against
his own superior,* held the Oregon statutes overbroad and
therefore void because they prohibited a civil servant from
becoming a candidate for *any* political office—state, federal,
or nonpartisan.

On virtually identical facts, the California Supreme
Court invalidated on grounds of overbreadth a San Francisco charter provision prohibiting any city or county
employee from becoming a candidate for public office.[103]
Similarly, a New Jersey court ruled in favor of a city fireman who was threatened with dismissal after running for
the city council in violation of an even more sweeping
fire-department rule prohibiting members of the department
from taking an active part in political contests. The court
struck down the rule, holding that the right to engage in
political activity is protected by the First Amendment, and
that the rule was overbroad and not justified by any
compelling state interest.[104]

Holding unconstitutional similar charter provisions, a
federal court stated that "[s]uch a broad prophylactic rule
nets more than the abuses it seeks to encompass," and that

the evils sought to be prevented could be expunged by narrower rules, such as conflict of interest rules, or leaves
of absence from employment while campaigning.[105] Observing that the charter provisions restricted the rights not
only of public employees but also of voters by limiting the
fields of candidates from whom the voters might choose,[106]
the court held that a regulation restricting First Amendment freedoms is invalid where it "prohibits activities
which may not be proscribed as well as activities which
may be proscribed," or where there is a "less drastic
means" by which the legitimate goal of the statute could
be achieved.[107] The court noted that although the *Mitchell*
decision had not been expressly overruled, its vitality had
been vitiated by the force of subsequent decisions.[108]

Other courts, relying on the Supreme Court's decision in
Mitchell, have held that a public employee may be forced
to relinquish his public employment if he becomes a
candidate for elective office. In 1961, the Florida Supreme
Court upheld the dismissal of a law professor at the University of Florida for violating a restriction against seeking
public office.[109] In 1969, a Wisconsin federal district court
sustained a narrower policy of the Wisconsin Department
of Natural Resources providing that "no employee shall
run for any *partisan* elective office. . . ."[110]

One court, although holding the "compelling-interest"
test applicable, upheld a statute prohibiting state employees
from running for compensated public office. The court
concluded that the legislature had a compelling interest in
obviating "the evils which necessarily follow when officers
or employes [sic] in the classified service of the state are
permitted to engage in political activity to the extent of
running for office."[111] The court thought the legislature
could conclude that campaigning would inevitably interfere
with the candidate's time, energy, and devotion to official
duties; that an employee seeking elective office could use
the prestige of the office he was seeking to gain special
treatment from his superiors; that his campaign activities
would promote or retard his advancement, and that he

might use his state employment to favor those who might aid him in his campaign.[112]

(4.) May a teacher constitutionally be required to take a leave of absence without pay while he campaigns for public office?

Yes. The courts have rejected challenges to rules requiring a teacher to take an unpaid leave of absence during the period of his campaign for public office. As one court put it, ". . . anyone who has been a candidate recognizes that political activity is apt to interfere with one's usual avocation [sic] and this fact, independent of any possible involvement of the school system in political controversies, affords a sound reason for a temporary severance of the candidate's connection with the schools."[113]

In one recent case, a teacher sought an injunction under the Civil Rights Act against enforcement of a school-board regulation which required him to take a leave of absence from the date of his qualification as a candidate for public office—in his case, the office of member of his own school board—until the day following election day. The campaign period was two weeks. The court held the regulation valid. Responding to the teacher's contention that there was no showing that his work was actually impaired, or that the campaign process otherwise rendered him incompetent or inefficient, the court stated:

> Any effort to measure a teacher's performance during a relatively short campaign period would be virtually impossible, and probably an exercise in futility as there would undoubtedly be requirements for hearings on the subject of incompetency, inefficiency, or failure to perform one's duty. It therefore appears to the Court that a regulation such as the one in question is the most appropriate way to handle a short-span matter such as this where, in the knowledge of all persons concerned, it is clearly apparent that a person engaged in a campaign for a public office will have his attention diverted to some extent from his primary activities.[114]

(5.) May a teacher constitutionally be forced to relinquish his teaching position if he serves as state legislator, city councilman or school-board member, or holds some other part-time elected public office?

The courts have not yet definitely answered this question. The issue is arising with increasing frequency, since hundreds of teachers serve in state legislatures and many others hold such local elective offices as alderman and city councilman. At present, however, it is unclear to what extent the Constitution gives a teacher who serves in such a part-time elected office the right to retain his teaching position.

On behalf of the teacher, it is argued that any law or policy which would force him to relinquish his teaching position must be judged by the "compelling state interest" test. Arguably, such a test is peculiarly appropriate where the restriction has the effect of preventing or discouraging a candidate elected by the voters from assuming office.[115] Moreover, "[a]ny unjustified discrimination in determining who may participate in political affairs . . . undermines the legitimacy of representative government."[116] As the Supreme Court has said in another context: "The presumption of constitutionality and the approval given 'rational' classifications in other types of enactments are based on an assumption that the institutions of state government are structured so as to represent fairly all the people. However, when the challenge to the statute is in effect a challenge of this basic assumption, the assumption can no longer serve as the basis for presuming constitutionality."[117]

If the compelling-interest test were adopted, the validity of the restriction in each case would turn on (1) the legitimacy of the interest asserted by the state; (2) whether the restriction is narrowly confined to further the state's interest; and (3) whether the state's interest is sufficiently compelling to warrant the infringement upon the teacher's constitutional freedom.[118]

Under such a test, for example, if the state or school board asserted that as an elected official the teacher would have a conflict of interest because he could affect his own salary and working conditions, the court would inquire into the legitimacy of the asserted conflict in terms of the precise relationship between the elected office and the teaching post. If the court determined that the requisite conflict existed, it would then decide whether there were other ways in which this problem could be met without infringing on the teacher's right, *e.g.*, by disqualifying him from voting where he had an interest, by requiring disclosure of his interest to the electorate, or by freezing his teaching salary during his term of elected office. The court also would ask whether the state's interest was compelling in light of such factors as the extent to which comparable restrictions had been placed on others similarly situated and the extent to which other jurisdictions had found it necessary to impose such restrictions.

No court has yet adopted this analysis. In one case an assistant superintendent in a Tennessee school district, whose function included the initial preparation of the annual school budget, claimed that his constitutional rights were violated by state conflict-of-interest statutes which, as construed by the state courts, barred him from receiving any salary as assistant superintendent so long as he held the post of alderman. The aldermanic post, to which he had been elected, carried a stipend of two hundred fifty dollars per annum.[119] Voters who had cast their ballots for him joined in the suit, contending that their right to vote had been rendered ineffective. A three-judge court was convened but dissolved itself for lack of a substantial federal question and the dissolution was upheld in a two-one decision by the U.S. Court of Appeals.[120]

Since his duties do not include preparation of the school budget, a teacher would appear to be in a stronger position to assert a constitutional right to hold part-time public office while retaining his position and salary with the school system, even where the responsibilities of the public office include actions affecting the school system. Thus, where a teacher at a state college in West Virginia was elected to the state legislature but was not permitted to take his seat because a provision of the West Virginia Constitution was construed to bar state employees from sitting in the legislature, a three-judge court was convened and proceeded to hear a federal constitutional challenge to the provision by the teacher and citizens who voted for him.[121]

The U.S. Supreme Court, however, recently dismissed an appeal from a Texas decision upholding the constitutionality of a state statute which, as interpreted, barred the comptroller from paying the salaries of six members of the faculty and staff of Texas A&M so long as they were serving concurrently as elected councilmen. Rejecting the employees' claim that the statute was repugnant to the equal-protection clause, the Texas court stated:

> The purpose of . . . [the statute] is to avoid the harm which may follow when State employees who serve on a merit basis become involved in the political process to the extent of holding an elective State office. It is a reasonable conclusion that campaigning for and holding an elective state office would interfere with the employee's time, energy and devotion to his official duties.[122]

The court pointed to a lower-court finding that a potential conflict of interest existed between the services of the employees to the Texas A&M system and their service as councilmen, citing evidence that they spent time on city matters while on duty at their college offices.

Another state court decided that a teacher elected to the state legislature did not have a federal constitutional right to demand a leave of absence limited to the periods of time that the legislature was in session or her attendance was required at committee meetings, since the school board reasonably could determine that the teacher's return in the middle of the semester would disrupt the orderly operation of the schools.[123]

(6.) May a state or school board constitutionally restrict the right of a teacher to campaign against his employing school board or superintendent?

The answer turns on whether, considering all the facts, the restriction is required to preserve the efficiency and integrity of the school system.

A teacher is vulnerable if he campaigns during school hours or on school grounds. Upholding the dismissal of a teacher for campaigning against his elected superintendent, the Supreme Court of Alaska relied in part upon the fact that the teacher had campaigned "during school hours on school premises. . . ."[124]

A teacher's participation in a school-board campaign during off-duty hours away from the school premises would not appear to have such a harmful impact upon the school system as to warrant the school board's interference. The composition of a school board is obviously a matter of "public concern" and a teacher's employment relationship with a board member normally is not, in the language of *Pickering*, the kind of close working relationship "for which it can persuasively be claimed that personal loyalty and confidence are necessary" to its proper functioning.[125]

Thus, although the California Supreme Court has suggested that "[a] strong case . . . can . . . be made for the view that permitting a public employee to run or campaign against his own superior has so disruptive an effect on the public service as to warrant restriction,"[126] the same court subsequently left open the question whether the working relationship between a nurse and members of the hospital board "was so immediate that the board might be considered her 'own superior'."[127]

A teacher's right to campaign against his elected superintendent may present a closer question. In a large school system, a superintendent may have more contact than a board member with an individual teacher, but probably not so much as to warrant a restriction upon the teacher's participation in a campaign against him. In *Pickering*, the Court sustained a teacher's right to publicly criticize his superintendent's methods of keeping from the taxpayers the real reason why additional tax revenues were being sought for the schools. The court noted that the teacher's employment relationship with the superintendent, though "to a somewhat lesser extent" than his relationship with the board, was not the kind of close working relationship which demanded personal loyalty and confidence.

In a small school system, a court might reach a different conclusion. Where there were only two schools, and thirty teachers in the system, and the superintendent dealt directly with all the teachers and "was in fact the school principal as well," a court held that the actions of teachers in attacking and attempting to oust the superintendent were not within the protective umbrella of *Pickering*. Rather, the court said, the teachers' actions "were directed toward a person with whom appellants would normally be in contact in the course of their daily work as teachers, and where a question of maintaining discipline by an immediate superior was involved."[128]

Even where particular campaign activity may constitutionally be prohibited, the ban may be unconstitutional if it is "overbroad." For example, the California Supreme Court found it unnecessary to decide the question whether a nurse's conduct in campaigning during off-duty hours to recall members of the hospital board could have been reached by a narrowly drawn statute or directive, holding that the restriction in question extended "beyond the area of permissible limitation. . . ."[129]

ASSOCIATION ACTIVITY

Union Activity

(1.) Do teachers have a constitutional right to belong to an employee organization?

Yes. Public employees—including teachers—have a Federal constitutional right to freedom of association derived from the First and Fourteenth Amendments to the United States Constitution. This includes the right to form and join labor organizations,[130] whether local or national.[131]

Teachers have a constitutional right not only to belong to an employee organization but also to assume a leadership role in the organization, including advocacy and persuasion in organizing the union, enlarging its membership, and expressing its views to employees and the public,[132] and representation of the organization in its negotiations with the school board. Moreover, ". . . a teacher may not be denied a teaching contract because of his actions in a professional association, regardless of how vigorous they are. . . ."[133] Where a school board failed to renew the contracts of nine teachers—among them the leaders of the union and some of its most active members—in retribution for their union activities, the board was held to violate the teachers' constitutional right to freedom of association.[134] Nor can a school board constitutionally deny tenure to a teacher because he is a union activist.[135]

A teacher, of course, is not immunized from termination or discipline "simply because he also serves as a negotiator in contract disputes with his employer."[136] Thus, "a school board has the authority to release any teacher who engages in activities which prove to be seriously detrimental to his classroom work, even where those activities are on behalf of a union or other association."[137] And a teacher who is a negotiator has no greater right than any other teacher to consider "his own view of what his professional responsibilities ought to be as the authoritative guide to the reasonableness of the rules and regulations" imposed by the school authorities.[138]

(2.) Does a teacher have a right to join an employee organization that engages in unlawful strikes or other illegal activity?

Yes. In *McLaughlin* v. *Tilendis*,[139] nontenured teachers sued school officials under the Civil Rights Act claiming that their employment had been terminated because of their union activities. Upholding their right to bring such a claim under the Act, the court ruled that "[u]nless there is some illegal intent, an individual's right to form and join a union is protected by the First Amendment."[140]

Responding to the contention that the union might engage in strikes or other activity injurious to the public interest, the court said that even if the union were "connected with unlawful activity," the bare fact of membership would not justify charging members with their organization's misdeeds. "A contrary rule would bite more deeply into associational freedom than is necessary to achieve legitimate state interests, thereby violating the First Amendment."[141]

(3.) Can a state or school board constitutionally ban membership by administrators or supervisors in an employee organization?

No. In 1969, a federal court invalidated a Florida law which barred all administrators and supervisors in the Palm Beach County school system from participation or membership in any organization which engaged in "the collective representation of members of the teaching profession with regard to terms, tenure or conditions of employment." The court held that in addition to denying equal protection of the laws to members of the teaching profession employed in Palm Beach County, the statute impinged upon freedoms of expression and association protected by the First and Fourteenth Amendments.[142]

(4.) Does a school board have a constitutional obligation to bargain collectively with an organization representing a majority of the teachers?

The question is not settled. Since teachers have the right under the Constitution "to associate for the purpose of collective bargaining,"[143] as well as to freedom of speech and petition, it has been argued that the school board has a corresponding duty to bargain in good faith with an organization representing a majority of the teachers, and to give that organization exclusive recognition in order to make the right and duty meaningful.

Most courts have rejected this contention. In one case, a federal district court held that a school board had such a constitutional duty, and temporarily halted school officials from bargaining individually with teachers. The appellate court, however, granted a motion to stay the injunction pending appeal. The court stated: "There is no question that the right of teachers to associate for the purpose of collective bargaining is a right protected by the First and Fourteenth Amendments to the Constitution. . . . But there is no constitutional duty to bargain collectively with an exclusive bargaining agent. Such duty, when imposed, is imposed by statute."[144]

Recently, however, a federal district court in Virginia refused to dismiss a complaint alleging that the refusal of the school board to meet and discuss conditions of employment with the Richmond Education Association, whose membership included most teachers in the district, and to recognize it as a representative of its members and the exclusive representative of the class it purported to represent, was unconstitutional. The plaintiffs alleged that they had a constitutional right as public sector employees to organize and associate for the purpose of collectively representing their employment interests, and that by stopping all dealings with the Association the board had effectively blunted the exercise of those rights. The court stated:

> The grant of approval to organize and associate without the corresponding grant of recognition may well be an empty and meaningless gesture on the part of the defendant School Board. . .[145]

The court concluded that "plaintiffs' allegation that the defendants' wrongful actions have a chilling effect upon the exercise of plaintiffs' First Amendment rights does indeed state a claim upon which relief, if due, can be granted."[146] In addition to denying the motion to dismiss, the court denied the defendants' motion for summary judgment.

(5.) Do teachers have a constitutionally protected right to strike?

The Supreme Court has indicated that within the concern of the First Amendment right of association are essential organizational activities which give an organization life and promote its fundamental purposes.[147] Arguably the strike is indispensable to the viability of a labor organization. As one federal judge has noted: "If the inherent purpose of a labor organization is to bring the workers' interests to bear on management, the right to strike is, historically and practically, an important means of effectuating that purpose. A union that never strikes, or which can make no credible threat to strike, may wither away in ineffectiveness."

Some judges, therefore, in concurring and dissenting opinions, have accepted the view that ". . . the right to strike is, at least, within constitutional concern and should not be discriminatorily abridged without substantial or 'compelling' justification."[148] One judge, expressing doubt about the validity of a flat ban on strikes by federal employees, pointed to the plaintiff union's arguments that not all federal services were "essential," and that some privately provided services fell into that category. He also noted that "in our mixed economic system of governmental and private enterprise, the line separating governmental from private functions may depend more on the accidents of history than on substantial differences in kind."[149]

Similar arguments were made by two judges on the Supreme Court of Indiana who dissented from a holding by the majority of the court that every strike by public employees, including teachers, is illegal and therefore enjoinable, regardless of how peaceful and nondisruptive it is. The dissenting judges concluded that it would violate the equal protection clause of the Fourteenth Amendment to treat a nondisruptive strike by public employees differently from a similar strike by private employees.[150]

Nevertheless, no court has yet held that public employees have a constitutional right to strike. Many decisions hold to the contrary.[151] And recently, the United States Supreme Court summarily affirmed a lower-court decision upholding the constitutionality of an absolute ban on strikes by federal employees.[152] While the significance of this decision—rendered without hearing oral argument and without written opinion—is not entirely clear,[153] it affords little comfort to public-employee organizations seeking judicial recognition of the constitutional right of their members to strike.

Other Associational Activity

(1.) May a state or school officials constitutionally forbid a teacher to be a member of a "subversive" organization as a condition of public employment?

No. Mere membership in such an organization is not sufficient grounds for discharge or exclusion from public employment.

In *Keyishian* v. *Board of Regents*,[154] teachers at the State University of New York attacked the constitutionality of a state law making communist party membership "prima-facie" evidence of disqualification for employment in the public school system. The Supreme Court struck down this provision insofar as it proscribed mere knowing membership in an organization found to be subversive "without any showing of specific intent to further . . . [its] unlawful aims. . . ."[155] The Court held the provision to be an unconstitutional interference with associational rights because of its "overbreadth."[156]

In 1969, Angela Davis was fired by the University of California because of her admitted membership in the Communist Party. The dismissal was based on resolutions of the University of California Regents adopted in the 1940s and 1950s, affirming the University's dedication to "search for truth in its full exposition," its commitment to the freedom of the human mind, and its responsibility to protect the University from those seeking to destroy that freedom. The resolutions—asserting that freedom was "menaced on a world-wide basis" by the Communist Party, which sought control of thought and expression, and that therefore membership in the party was incompatible with teaching and the search for truth—directed the University administration to terminate any person found to be a member of the party.

Four California taxpayers brought suit for a declaratory judgment that the resolutions violated both the Federal and state constitutions, and that implementation of the resolutions by the expenditure of tax monies was an impermissible use of public funds. Angela Davis was permitted to intervene. The trial court held that the resolutions violated the First and Fourteenth Amendments to the Federal Constitution, as well as provisions of the state constitution, "because they automatically excluded from faculty employment by the University . . . solely by virtue of such membership, any person who is a member of the Communist Party." Accordingly, the court declared illegal any expenditure of funds to implement any of the resolutions. On appeal, the court of appeals concluded it was "manifest" that the judgment was sustained by the reasoning of *Keyishian* and other cases.[157]

(2.) May a state or school officials constitutionally forbid a teacher to associate with persons holding unconventional social views?

No, at least absent a showing that the association renders the teacher unfit to teach or threatens to impair the effective operation of the school system.

For example, teachers on occasion have been dismissed or refused reappointment because of their membership in a nudist colony.[158] Such terminations are of doubtful constitutionality. One federal court held unconstitutional, as an infringement upon his First Amendment freedom of association, the Baltimore Police Department's denial of an application for employment as a probationary patrolman on the ground that the applicant was a practicing nudist.[159] The First and Fourteenth Amendments, the court held, protect the "right to associate with any person of one's choosing for the purpose of advocating and promoting legitimate, albeit controversial, political, social or economic views."[160] The court held that the defendant police commissioner had "failed to show by clear and convincing evidence such a paramount governmental interest as would justify an intrusion upon plaintiff's First Amendment right, and his policy of total exclusion of all nudists is arbitrary and capricious."[161]

(3.) May a state or school authorities constitutionally compel a teacher to disclose his associational relationships as a condition of public employment?

Only when disclosure is justified by a compelling state interest. The Supreme Court has recognized "the vital relationship between freedom to associate and privacy in one's associations. . . ."[162] Thus, it has held that absent a compelling governmental interest, the First Amendment protects individuals from compulsory disclosure of their associational relationships. For example, absent such a compelling interest, one may not be exposed for his membership in such groups as the National Association for the Advancement of Colored People.[163]

It is not clear to what extent, if at all, states or school authorities may compel disclosure of a teacher's associational ties in pursuit of an inquiry into the qualifications of their teachers. In *Shelton* v. *Tucker*, [164] the Supreme Court ruled unconstitutional an Arkansas law requiring teachers, as a condition of employment in a state-supported school or college, to file annually an affidavit listing every organization to which they had belonged or contributed. The Court ruled that the disclosure requirement, with its "unlimited and indiscriminate sweep," went "far beyond what might be justified in the exercise of the State's legitimate inquiry into the fitness and competency of its teachers," and impermissibly inhibited the teachers' right of free association.[165]

In *Shelton*, the Court cited, among other considerations, the fact that Arkansas was a nontenure state, where a teacher's continued employment depended on the discretion of the school authorities to renew his one-year contract; and where no provision was made for notice, charges, hearing, or opportunity to explain. It is not clear to what extent the decision would protect tenured teachers, whose employment cannot be terminated except for just cause and then only after notice and hearing, from similar disclosure requirements. Nor is it clear to what extent *Shelton* shields applicants for employment from such requirements.

(4.) May a teacher be required by a legislative committee to disclose his associational relationships on pain of contempt or criminal punishment?

Not if the teacher asserts a proper claim of privilege against self-incrimination (see Chapter VIII).

Some teachers also have urged that they cannot constitutionally be subjected to such interrogation consistently with their constitutional right of free association. Under current law, however, legislative committees may, without violating the Constitution, investigate an individual's associational relationships if acting pursuant to a legislative authorization justified by a compelling state interest.[166] The Supreme Court has held that teachers are not immune from such exposure. In *Barenblatt* v. *United States*, [167] a teacher declined to answer questions of a subcommittee of the House Committee on Un-American Activities concerning his prior affiliation with communist organizations while he was a graduate student and teaching fellow at the University of Michigan. He contended that the academic profession should have a special privilege to withhold information regarding associational activities. The court rejected this argument, stating that Congress is not "precluded from interrogating a witness merely because he is a teacher."[168]

LOYALTY PROGRAMS

Loyalty oaths for teachers have old roots. In colonial times, teachers who refused to swear allegiance to the Revolutionary government or who publicly proclaimed loyalty to England suffered financial or even bodily harm. Some were driven out of the country, including President Cooper of Columbia, who fled half-dressed over the college fence, escaping to a British sloop.[169] "Patriotic" oaths commonly have been required of teachers in other times of stress—for example, during the Civil War. The practice became widespread during and after the First World War, when a number of states enacted loyalty-oath legislation[170] and also during the McCarthy period, when loyalty oaths were used as devices to insure that the teachers of our impressionable youth were "one hundred percent Americans."

Teachers have objected to loyalty-oath requirements on a number of grounds. Such oaths are criticized as futile since any person against whom society needs protection is unlikely to have scruples against subscribing to the oath and breaking it. It is also contended that the general nature of the typical oath permits interested pressure groups to suppress teacher questioning of orthodox views, and that such suppression is its real purpose.

In a recent spate of litigation teachers have challenged requirements that they participate in what one court has termed "a peculiar sub-species of loyalty oaths"[171]—the pledge of allegiance to the flag—conceived in 1892 as a voluntary and recommended patriotic exercise for the quadricentennial celebration of Columbus Day and not made obligatory until 1898, one day after commencement of the Spanish-American War, when New York became the first state to make the pledge a mandatory requirement.[172]

(1.) May a teacher constitutionally be required to sign a loyalty oath as a condition of public employment?

Not unless the oath is properly limited in accordance with judicial rulings sharply curtailing the type of oath that may be required.

The Supreme Court and lower federal courts have struck down, as violations of First Amendment guarantees of freedom of speech and association, requirements that a teacher foreswear membership in a "subversive" organization or the abstract advocacy of subversion, as well as oaths which are so vague and uncertain as to deter protected speech or association. These courts have invalidated requirements that a teacher swear or affirm that:

(a.) he has never lent his "aid, support, advice, counsel or influence to the Communist Party";[173]

(b.) he does not advocate the overthrow of the government and is not a member of an organization that he knows advocates such overthrow;[174]

(c.) he is not and will not knowingly become a member of an organization that advocates the overthrow of our constitutional form of government;[175]

(d.) he is not a member of an organization advocating overthrow of the government by violence or other unlawful means; is not affiliated directly or indirectly with the Communist Party or other subversive organization, and has not been a member of such an organization within the preceding five years;[176]

(e.) he is not engaged "in one way or another" in an attempt to overthrow the government by force;[177]

(f.) he will "by precept and example promote respect for the flag and the institutions of the United States of America and the State . . . , reverence for law and order and undivided allegiance to the government of the United States";[178] and

(g.) he will "refrain from directly or indirectly subscribing to or teaching any theory of government or economics or of social relations which is inconsistent with the fundamental principles of patriotism and high ideals of Americanism."[179]

The Supreme Court has upheld a requirement that, as a condition of public employment, a teacher take an oath to "uphold the Constitution of the United States and of the State . . . and . . . faithfully perform the duties of the position upon which" he is about to enter.[180] The Court also has sustained a statute imposing on each public employee the duty to swear or affirm that he will "oppose the overthrow of the government of the United States of America or of . . . [the State] by force, violence, or by an illegal or unconstitutional method."[181]

(2.) Can a teacher constitutionally be required to swear or affirm that he does not or will not assert the right to strike against the government or that he does not belong to any organization which he knows asserts such a right?

Probably not. Such an employment oath for federal employees was struck down by a federal court on the ground that under the First Amendment a public employee has a

constitutional right to argue for the right to strike and to
petition for legislative changes conferring such a right.[182]

**(3.) Can a teacher constitutionally be required to salute
the flag or to lead his class in, or recite, the pledge of
allegiance?**

Under the weight of authority, a teacher has a constitutional right to refuse to obey such a requirement.

In a recent Connecticut case, for example, a teacher
dismissed for refusing to lead her class in the pledge
objected that the phrase "with liberty and justice for all"
was an untrue statement of present fact and "was not a
pledge to work for something because it doesn't say
that."[183] Thus, she arranged for a student to lead the class
in the pledge, while she remained seated at her desk with
her head bowed. A federal court issued a preliminary
injunction reinstating her, stating:

> There is no question but that Mrs. Hanover's refusal to
> recite or lead recitation of the Pledge of Allegiance is
> a form of expression protected by the first amend-
> ment which may not be forbidden at the risk of los-
> ing her job. It does not matter that her expression
> took the form of silence. . . . Nor is it relevant to
> inquire whether her expression is attributable to a
> doubtful grammatical construction of the Pledge of
> Allegiance or outright disagreement with it.[184]

The court held that the teacher's behavior had not resulted
in disruption of school activities or interfered with the
rights of other teachers or students, and that it was imma-
terial whether some of her students, who also refrained
from recitation of the pledge, were persuaded to do so
because of her conduct.[185]

In another case, a high-school French teacher in New
York City was suspended for failure, after warnings by
his supervisors, to lead or participate as a homeroom
teacher in the pledge. Dismissal charges were preferred by
the superintendent based on the incident and the board of

education appointed a lawyer—a former President of the Association of the Bar of the City of New York—to serve as an independent trial examiner.

The teacher testified that prior to his decision to take no part in the flag services, he had led his homeroom class in the pledge with "very great violence" to himself. He felt "one should not have to prove one's loyalty in words." He objected to "many of the terms of the Pledge"—in particular to the words "one Nation under God, indivisible, with liberty and justice for all." In reciting the pledge, he had added, "for all who fight for it" to "liberty and justice." He had a "notion" that the country is not one country indivisible—that to say so is embarrassing and hypocritical. He regarded the pledge as "coercive" and felt that daily repetition drained it of meaning.

The examiner's report recommended to the board that the teacher be reinstated as a French teacher without a homeroom assignment or that a student be permitted to lead the pledge. Absent an administrative disposition of this sort, the examiner concluded, a court would hold that the teacher's constitutional rights had been infringed. The examiner stated that "the Board is required . . . to adopt means for promoting student patriotism that do not impair the personal liberties of teachers."[186] The decision of the examiner subsequently was relied upon by a federal court in upholding the right of students to remain seated during the pledge of allegiance.[187]

Recently the highest court of Maryland invalidated a Maryland law requiring all students and teachers, except those who objected for religious reasons, to stand, salute the flag, and recite in unison the pledge of allegiance. The law was successfully challenged by a teacher and his son, a high-school student. The father claimed that he would refuse to engage in a mandatory flag salute ceremony, not for religious reasons but because he could not "in good conscience" force patriotism upon his classes and because he believed such a requirement eliminated his right to freely express his own loyalty to the United States. The court ruled that the statute infringed upon the free-speech rights of the teacher and his son.[188]

NOTES

1. *See* Metzger, "The Age of the University" in R. Hofstadter and W. Metzger, *The Development of Academic Freedom in the United States* 388-90, 400-06 (1955); *Developments in the Law,—Academic Freedom,* 81 Harv. L. Rev. 1045, 1048 (1968).

2. H. Beale, *A History of Freedom of Teaching In American Schools* 237 (1941).

3. *Id.* at 149.

4. *Id.* at 237-42.

5. *Id.* at 240.

6. 391 U.S. 563 (1968).

7. *Id.* at 570 (emphasis added).

8. *Id.* at 569-70.

9. *Id.* at 570. *Compare Moore* v. *Winfield City Board of Educ.,* 452 F.2d 726, 727-28 (5th Cir. 1971).

10. H. Beale, *A History of Freedom of Teaching in American Schools* 570 n.3 (1941).

11. *Id.* at 570.

12. *Id.* at 574 (emphasis added).

13. 391 U.S. at 571-72.

14. *McGee* v. *Richmond Unified School District,* 306 F.Supp. 1052, 1053 (N.D. Cal. 1969). *See also Armstead* v. *Starkville Municipal Separate School District,* 331 F.Supp. 567 (N.D. Miss. 1971). *Cf. In re Gioglio,* 104 N.J. Super. 88, 248 A.2d 570 (1968).

15. *Smith* v. *Losee,* Civil No. C-283-69 (D. Utah Jan. 27, 1972) p. 7, 4 College Law Bull. 41 (1972).

16. *Id.* at 8.

17. *Garcia* v. *City of Cheyenne,* Civil No. 5536 (D. Wyo. Aug. 31, 1971) p. 4.

18. *Swaaley* v. *United States,* 376 F.2d 857 (Ct. Cl. 1967).

19. *Puentes* v. *Board of Educ.,* 24 N.Y. 2d 996, 250 N.E. 2d 232, 302 N.Y.S. 2d 824 (1969). *See also United States* v. *United States District Court,* 40 U.S.L.W. 4761, 4766 (U.S. June 19, 1972) ("[P]rivate dissent, no less than open public discourse, is essential to our free society").

20. 391 U.S. at 569-70.

21. *Id.* at 570.

22. *Id.* at 570 n.3.
23. *Watts* v. *Seward School Board,* 454 P.2d 732, 735 (Alaska 1969), *cert. denied,* 397 U.S. 921 (1970).
24. *Ibid. See also Ahern* v. *Board of Educ.,* 327 F.Supp. 1391, 1396-97 (D. Neb. 1971), *aff'd,* 456 F.2d 399 (8th Cir. 1972). *Cf. Lefcourt* v. *Legal Aid Society,* 312 F.Supp. 1105, 1112-13 (S.D.N.Y. 1970), *aff'd,* 445 F.2d 1150 (2d Cir. 1971), where the court upheld the dismissal of a legal aid society attorney whose criticism of his superiors had a "definite impact on the internal operation of the society" and threatened the "confidence and close working relationship" necessary to the effective operation of the society.
25. *Roberts* v. *Lake Central School Corp.,* 317 F.Supp. 63, 64 (N.D. Ind. 1970).
26. 393 U.S. 503 (1969).
27. *Id.* at 509.
28. *Id.* at 513.
29. *Ibid.*
30. *Grayned* v. *City of Rockford,* 40 U.S.L.W. 4881, 4885 (U.S. June 27, 1972); *Healy* v. *James,* 40 U.S.L.W. 4887, 4894 (U.S. June 27, 1972).
31. *Jones* v. *Battles,* 315 F.Supp. 601, 607 (D. Conn. 1970).
32. *Chase* v. *Fall Mountain Regional School District,* 330 F.Supp. 388 (D. N.H. 1971).
33. *Testerman* v. *Lake Forest Board of Educ.,* C.A. No. 203 (Super. Ct. Del., Kent County Dec. 17, 1971) p. 8; *Cf. Merkle* v. *McGraw,* No. 13654 MP-83, Decision No. 9582-B (Wis. Empl. Rel. Comm'n, Aug. 30, 1971) pp. 6, 9-10. *Compare Gieringer* v. *Center School District,* Civil Action No. 18515-2 (W.D. Mo. May 24, 1972) pp. 6-7.
34. *Puentes* v. *Board of Educ.,* 24 N.Y. 2d 996, 999, 250 N.E. 2d 232, 233, 302 N.Y.S. 2d 824, 826 (1969).
35. *Jones* v. *Battles,* 315 F.Supp. 601 (D. Conn. 1970). *Cf. Palo Verde Unified School District* v. *Hensey,* 88 Cal. Rptr. 570, 575, 9 Cal. App. 3d 967, 974 (1970).
36. *Duke* v. *North Texas State University,* 338 F.Supp. 990, 997 (E.D. Tex. 1971).
37. *Brukiewa* v. *Police Commissioner,* 257 Md. 36, 263 A.2d 210 (1970). *Compare Wilderman* v. *Nelson,* 335 F.Supp. 1381 (E.D. Mo. 1971) (discharge of probationary welfare caseworker for writing interoffice memorandum criticizing the "system" as "rotten" and acknowledging an intent to

work against its efficient operation upheld against contention that memorandum was protected speech).

38. 391 U.S. 563, 572 n.4.
39. *Tepedino* v. *Dumpson*, 24 N.Y. 2d 705, 709, 249 N.E. 2d 751, 753, 301 N.Y.S. 2d 967, 968 (1969).
40. 24 N.Y. 2d at 709, 249 N.E. 2d at 752, 301 N.Y.S. 2d at 969.
41. See answer to previous question.
42. *Armstead* v. *Starkville Municipal Separate School District,* 331 F.Supp. 567 (N.D. Miss. 1971).
43. *Developments in the Law—Academic Freedom,* 81 Harv. L. Rev. 1045, 1069 (1968).
44. *Downs* v. *Conway School District,* 328 F.Supp. 338 (E.D. Ark. 1971).
45. See answer to question 7.
46. *Jackson* v. *United States,* 428 F.2d 844, 846 (Ct. Cl. 1970).
47. *Swaaley* v. *United States,* 376 F.2d 857 (Ct. Cl. 1967). *See also Burkett* v. *United States,* 402 F.2d 1002, 1008 (Ct. Cl. 1968).
48. *Tepedino* v. *Dumpson,* 24 N.Y. 2d 705, 249 N.E. 2d 751, 301 N.Y.S. 2d 967 (1969).
49. See answer to question 7.
50. *Cf. Iannarelli* v. *Morton,* 327 F.Supp. 873, 888 (E.D. Pa. 1971).
51. *Long* v. *Board of Educ.,* 331 F.Supp. 193, 197 (E.D. Mo. 1971), *aff'd,* 456 F.2d 1058 (8th Cir. 1972). *See also Murphy* v. *Facendia,* 307 F.Supp. 353, 355 (D. Colo. 1969).
52. *Murray* v. *Vaughn,* 300 F.Supp. 688, 705 (D. R.I. 1969), quoting *New York Times* v. *Sullivan,* 376 U.S. 254, 270 (1961). *See also Murray* v. *Blatchford,* 307 F.Supp. 1038, 1051 (D. R.I. 1969).
53. *Rainey* v. *Jackson State College,* 435 F.2d 1031 (5th Cir. 1970).
54. *Jervey* v. *Martin,* 336 F.Supp. 1350 (W.D. Va. 1972). *See also Council* v. *Donovan,* 40 Misc. 2d 744, 750, 244 N.Y.S. 2d 199, 205 (1963) (a teacher's license could not be cancelled "because of . . . his scruples against nuclear warfare"); *Bekiaris* v. *Board of Educ.,* 6 Cal. 3d 575, 100 Cal. Rptr. 16, 493 P.2d 480 (1972).
55. *Kay* v. *Board of Higher Educ.,* 173 Misc. 943, 18 N.Y.S. 2d 821 (1940), *aff'd without opinion,* 259 App. Div. 879, 20 N.Y.S. 2d 1016 (1940). The Supreme Court in *Picker-*

FREEDOM OF SPEECH 97

ing did imply that there might be a case in which a teacher's out-of-class public statements were "so without foundation as to call into question his fitness to perform his duties in the classroom." In such a case, the Court said, "the statements would merely be evidence of the teacher's general competence, or lack thereof, and not an independent basis for dismissal." *Pickering* v. *Board of Educ.*, 391 U.S. 563, 573 n.5. See criticism of this statement in Van Alstyne, *The Constitutional Rights of Teachers and Professors,* 1970 Duke L. J., 841, 853-54.

56. *Rozman* v. *Elliott*, 335 F.Supp. 1086, 1097 (D. Neb. 1971).

57. *Id.* at 1098.

58. *Blevins* v. *University of North Carolina*, No. C-21-D-70 (M.D.N.C. Sept. 8, 1971) pp. 8-9.

59. *Id.* at 9-10.

60. *Cf. Perry* v. *Sindermann*, 40 U.S.L.W. 5087, 5088-89 (U.S. June 29, 1972).

61. *Tinker* v. *Des Moines Community School District*, 393 U.S. 503, 506 (1969).

62. *Los Angeles Teachers Union* v. *Los Angeles City Board of Educ.*, 71 Cal. 2d 551, 78 Cal. Rptr. 723, 455 P.2d 827 (1969).

63. *Downs* v. *Conway School District*, 328 F.Supp. 338 (E.D. Ark. 1971).

64. *Long* v. *Board of Educ.*, 331 F.Supp. 193 (E.D. Mo. 1971), *aff'd*, 456 F.2d 1058 (8th Cir. 1972); *Murphy* v. *Facendia*, 307 F.Supp. 353, 354 (D. Colo. 1969).

65. *Tinker* v. *Des Moines Community School District*, 393 U.S. 503, 508 (1969).

66. *Los Angeles Teachers Union* v. *Los Angeles City Board of Educ.*, 71 Cal. 2d 551, 559, 78 Cal. Rptr. 723, 728, 455 P.2d 827, 832 (1969).

67. 71 Cal. 2d at 558, 78 Cal. Rptr. at 727, 455 P. 2d at 831.

68. *Reed* v. *Board of Educ.*, 333 F.Supp. 816 (E.D. Mo. 1971).

69. *Friedman* v. *Union Free School District No. 1*, 314 F.Supp. 223, 226-27 (E.D.N.Y. 1970), quoting from *Tinker* v. *Des Moines Community School District*, 393 U.S. 503, 506 (1969).

70. *Friedman* v. *Union Free School District No. 1*, 314 F.Supp. 223, 227 (E.D. N.Y. 1970).

71. *Id.* at 228.

72. *Pickings* v. *Bruce*, 430 F.2d 595 (8th Cir. 1970).

73. *E.g., Scoville* v. *Board of Educ.,* 425 F.2d 10 (7th Cir. 1970), *cert. denied,* 400 U.S. 826 (1970); *Antonelli* v. *Hammond,* 308 F.Supp. 1329 (D. Mass. 1970); *Zucker* v. *Panitz,* 299 F.Supp. 102 (S.D.N.Y. 1969). *But see Eisner* v. *Stamford Board of Educ.,* 440 F.2d 803 (2d Cir. 1971).

74. *Developments in the Law—Academic Freedom,* 81 Harv. L. Rev. 1045, 1069 (1968). *See Holden* v. *Finch,* 446 F.2d 1311, 1316 (D.C. Cir. 1971).

75. 364 F.2d 177 (4th Cir. 1966), *cert. denied,* 385 U.S. 1003 (1967).

76. *Rackley* v. *School District No. 5,* 258 F.Supp. 676 (D. S.C. 1966); *Williams* v. *Sumter School District No. 2,* 255 F.Supp. 397 (D.S.C. 1966); *Armstead* v. *Starkville Municipal Separate School District,* 331 F.Supp. 567 (N.D. Miss. 1971). *See also Rosenfield* v. *Malcolm,* 65 Cal. 2d 559, 55 Cal. Rptr. 505, 421 P.2d 697 (1967).

77. *Armstead* v. *Starkville Municipal Separate School District,* 331 F.Supp. 567 (N.D. Miss. 1971). *See also Iannarelli* v. *Morton,* 327 F.Supp. 873, 880 (E.D. Pa. 1971).

78. *James* v. *West Virginia Board of Regents,* 322 F.Supp. 217, 231 (S.D. W. Va. 1971), *aff'd,* 448 F.2d 785 (4th Cir. 1971).

79. *Holden* v. *Finch,* 446 F.2d 1311, 1316 (D.C. Cir. 1971).

80. *Ibid; Robbins* v. *Board of Educ.,* 313 F.Supp. 642, 647 (N.D. Ill. 1970).

81. *United Public Workers* v. *Mitchell,* 330 U.S. 75, 94-95 (1947); *Sweezy* v. *New Hampshire,* 354 U.S. 234, 250 (1957). *See also White* v. *Snear,* 313 F.Supp. 1100, 1103 (E.D. Pa. 1970); *Minielly* v. *State,* 242 Ore. 490, 499, 411 P.2d 69, 73 (1966); *Fort* v. *Civil Service Comm'n,* 61 Cal. 2d 331, 337, 38 Cal. Rptr. 625, 628-29, 392 P.2d 385, 388 (1964); *DeStefano* v. *Wilson,* 96 N.J. Super. 592, 597-98, 233 A.2d 682, 685 (1967).

82. 330 U.S. 75 (1947). *See also Oklahoma* v. *United States Civil Service Comm'n,* 330 U.S. 127 (1947).

83. *See Northern Virginia Regional Park Authority* v. *U.S. Civil Service Comm'n,* 437 F.2d 1346, 1351 (4th Cir. 1971) and cases cited.

84. *E.g., Shapiro* v. *Thompson,* 394 U.S. 618, 634, 638 (1969); *Sherbert* v. *Verner,* 374 U.S. 398, 406-07 (1963).

85. *Perry* v. *Sindermann,* 40 U.S.L.W. 5087, 5088 (U.S. June 29, 1972) and cases cited.

86. *Fort* v. *Civil Service Comm'n,* 61 Cal. 2d 331, 338, 38 Cal. Rptr. 625, 629, 392 P.2d 385, 389 (1964).

87. *Montgomery* v. *White*, 320 F.Supp. 303, 304 (E.D. Tex. 1969).

88. *Ibid.*

89. *Ibid.*

90. 448 F.2d 456, 470 (5th Cir. 1971).

91. *Id.* at 471.

92. *Id.* at 472.

93. *Id.* at 474.

94. *Id.* at 475.

95. *Mancuso* v. *Taft*, 341 F.Supp. 574, 575 (D.R.I. 1972).

96. *Id.* at 582.

97. *Id.* at 576-77.

98. *Bagley* v. *Washington Township Hospital District*, 65 Cal. 2d 499, 510-11, 55 Cal. Rptr. 401, 409, 421 P.2d 409, 417 (1966).

99. *Hobbs* v. *Thompson*, 448 F.2d 456, 471 (5th Cir. 1971).

100. *Bagley* v. *Washington Township Hospital District*, 65 Cal. 2d 499, 510, 55 Cal. Rptr. 401, 409, 421 P.2d 409, 417 (1966).

101. *Minielly* v. *State*, 242 Ore. 490, 499, 411 P.2d 69, 73 (1966).

102. 242 Ore. at 507, 411 P.2d at 77.

103. *Kinnear* v. *San Francisco*, 68 Cal. 2d 341, 38 Cal. Rptr. 631, 392 P.2d 391 (1964).

104. *DeStefano* v. *Wilson*, 96 N.J. Super. 592, 233 A.2d 682 (1967). *See also Fort* v. *Civil Service Comm'n*, 61 Cal. 2d 331, 38 Cal. Rptr. 625, 392 P.2d 385 (1964); *Bagley* v. *Washington Township Hospital District*, 65 Cal. 2d 499, 55 Cal. Rptr. 401, 421 P.2d 409 (1966).

105. *Mancuso* v. *Taft*, 341 F.Supp. 574, 583 (D.R. I. 1972).

106. *Id.* at 581.

107. *Id.* at 579.

108. *Id.* at 581.

109. *Jones* v. *Board of Control*, 131 So.2d 713 (Fla. 1961).

110. *Wisconsin State Employees Ass'n* v. *Wisconsin Natural Resources Board*, 298 F.Supp. 339, 342 (W.D. Wis 1969) (emphasis added).

111. *Johnson* v. *State Civil Service Dep't*, 280 Minn. 61, 66, 157 N.W. 2d 747, 751 (1968).

112. 280 Minn. at 66-67, 157 N.W. 2d at 751-52.

113. *School City* v. *Sigler*, 219 Ind. 9, 13, 36 N.E.2d 760, 762 (1941). *Accord, Chatham* v. *Johnson*, 195 So.2d 62 (Miss. 1967).

114. *Conrad* v. *Letson,* Civil Action File No. 13143 (N.D. Ga. May 12, 1971) p. 3.

115. *See Williams* v. *Rhodes,* 393 U.S. 23, 30-31 (1968). *See also Socialist Workers Party* v. *Rockefeller,* 314 F.Supp. 984 (S.D. N.Y. 1970), *aff'd* 400 U.S. 806 (1970).

116. *Kramer* v. *Union Free School District,* 395 U.S. 621, 626 (1969).

117. *Id.* at 628. *See also Stapleton* v. *Clerk for City of Inkster,* 311 F.Supp. 1187, 1190 (E.D. Mich. 1970); *Carter* v. *Dies,* 321 F.Supp. 1358, 1361 (N.D. Tex. 1970), *aff'd sub nom* 405, U.S. 134 (1972).

118. *See United States* v. *Robel,* 389 U.S. 258 (1967); *Keyishian* v. *Board of Regents,* 385 U.S. 589 (1967); *Aptheker* v. *Secretary of State,* 378 U.S. 500 (1964); *Kramer* v. *Union Free School District,* 395 U.S. 621 (1969).

119. *City of Kingsport* v. *Lay,* 459 S.W.2d 786, 787 (Ct. of App. Tenn. 1970).

120. *Lay* v. *City of Kingsport,* 454 F.2d 345 (6th Cir. 1972), *petition for cert. filed,* 41 U.S.L.W. 3009 (U.S. May 22, 1972) (No. 71-1524).

121. *Wilson* v. *Moore,* Civil Action No. 72-G-f (N.D. W.Va. Feb. 10, 1972) (order convening three-judge court).

122. *Boyett* v. *Calvert,* 467 S.W.2d 205, 210 (Tex. Civ. App. 1971), *appeal dismissed for want of a substantial federal question,* 40 U.S.L.W. 3483 (U.S. April 3, 1972).

123. *Hawkins* v. *Mineral County School District,* No. 4337 (Fifth Judicial District Court, Nev., Mineral County July 6, 1971) pp. 11-12.

124. *Watts* v. *Seward School Board,* 454 P.2d 732, 735 (Alaska 1969), *cert. denied,* 397 U.S. 921 (1970).

125. *Pickering* v. *Board of Educ.,* 391 U.S. 563, 570 (1968).

126. *Fort* v. *Civil Service Comm'n,* 61 Cal. 2d 331, 338, 38 Cal. Rptr. 625, 629, 392 P.2d 385, 389 (1964).

127. *Bagley* v. *Washington Township Hospital District,* 65 Cal. 2d 499, 508, 55 Cal. Rptr. 401, 408, 421 P.2d 409, 416 (1966).

128. *Watts* v. *Seward School Board,* 454 P.2d 732, 735 (Alaska 1969), *cert. denied,* 397 U.S. 921 (1970).

129. *Bagley* v. *Washington Township Hospital District,* 65 Cal. 2d 499, 511, 55 Cal. Rptr. 401, 409, 421 P.2d 409, 417 (1966).

130. *McLaughlin* v. *Tilendis,* 398 F.2d 287 (7th Cir. 1968); *AFSCME* v. *Woodward,* 406 F.2d 137 (8th Cir. 1969); *Orr* v. *Thorpe,* 427 F.2d 1129 (5th Cir. 1970); *Pred* v.

Board of Public Instruction, 415 F.2d 851 (5th Cir. 1969); *Indianapolis Educ. Ass'n* v. *Lewallen*, 72 LRRM 2071, 2072 (7th Cir. 1969); *Hanover Township Federation of Teachers* v. *Hanover Community School Corp.*, 318 F.Supp. 757 (N.D. Ind. 1970), *aff'd*, 457 F.2d 456 (7th Cir. 1972); *Atkins* v. *City of Charlotte*, 296 F.Supp. 1068 (W.D. N.C. 1969); *Melton* v. *City of Atlanta*, 324 F.Supp. 315 (N.D. Ga. 1971); *Beauboeuf* v. *Delgado College*, 303 F.Supp. 861, 864 n.2 (E.D. La. 1969), *aff'd*, 428 F.2d 470 (5th Cir. 1970); *City of Springfield* v. *Clouse*, 356 Mo. 1239, 1246-47, 206 S.W.2d 539, 542 (1947).

131. *Atkins* v. *City of Charlotte*, 296 F.Supp. 1068, 1077 (W.D. N.C. 1969).

132. *Hanover Township Federation of Teachers* v. *Hanover Community School Corp.*, 457 F.2d, 456, 460 (7th Cir. 1972).

133. *Lee* v. *Smith*, GERR No. 383, B-15, B-16 (E.D. Va. 1971).

134. *Hanover Township Federation of Teachers* v. *Hanover Community School Corp.*, 318 F.Supp. 757 (N.D. Ind. 1970), *aff'd.* 457 F.2d 456 (7th Cir. 1972).

135. *Tischler* v. *Board of Educ.*, 37 A.D.2d 261, 323 N.Y.S. 2d 508 (1971).

136. *Simard* v. *Board of Educ.*, Civil No. 14-379 (D. Conn. July 30, 1971) p. 16.

137. *Hanover Township Federation of Teachers* v. *Hanover Community School Corp.*, 318 F.Supp. 757, 763 (N.D. Ind. 1970).

138. *Simard* v. *Board of Educ.*, Civil No. 14-379 (D. Conn. July 30, 1971) p. 16.

139. 398 F.2d 287 (7th Cir. 1968).

140. *Id.* at 289.

141. *Ibid.*

142. *Orr* v. *Thorp*, 308 F.Supp. 1369 (S.D. Fla. 1969).

143. *Indianapolis Educ. Ass'n* v. *Lewallen*, 72 LRRM 2071, 2072 (7th Cir. 1969). *See also United Federation of Postal Clerks* v. *Blount*, 325 F.Supp. 879, 883 (D.D.C. 1971), *aff'd*, 404 U.S. 802 (1971).

144. *Indianapolis Educ. Ass'n* v. *Lewallen*, 72 LRRM 2071, 2072 (7th Cir. 1969). *See also Hanover Township Federation of Teachers* v. *Hanover Community School Corp.*, 457 F.2d 456 (7th Cir. 1972); *Atkins* v. *City of Charlotte*, 296 F.Supp. 1068, 1077 (W.D. N.C. 1969); *Newport*

News F.F.H. Local 794 v. *City of Newport News*, 339 F.Supp. 13 (E.D. Va. 1972); *Broward County Classroom Teachers Ass'n* v. *Broward County Board of Public Instruction*, No. 70-1520-Civ-JLK (S.D. Fla. May 8, 1972); *Cf. Beauboeuf* v. *Delgado College*, 303 F.Supp. 861 (E.D. La. 1969), *aff'd*, 428 F.2d 470 (5th Cir. 1970).

145. *Richmond Educ. Ass'n* v. *Crockford*, Civil Action No. 372-71-R (E.D. Va. June 14, 1972) p. 2.

146. *Id.* at 3

147. *Williams* v. *Rhodes*, 393 U.S. 23 (1968); *United Mine Workers* v. *Illinois State Bar Ass'n*, 389 U.S. 217 (1967).

148. *United Federation of Postal Clerks* v. *Blount*, 325 F.Supp. 879, 885 (D.D.C. 1971) (Wright, J., concurring), *aff'd*, 404 U.S. 802 (1971).

149. *Id.* at 885-86.

150. *Anderson Federation of Teachers* v. *School City*, 252 Ind. 558, 251 N.E.2d 15 (1969), *cert. denied*, 399 U.S. 928 (1970).

151. *See, e.g., Anderson Federation of Teachers* v. *School City*, 252 Ind. 558, 251 N.E.2d 15 (1969), *cert. denied*, 399 U.S. 928 (1970) and cases cited at 17; *United Federation of Postal Clerks* v. *Blount*, 325 F.Supp. 879 (D. D.C. 1971) and cases cited at 882.

152. *United Federation of Postal Clerks* v. *Blount*, 404 U.S. 802 (1971).

153. *See, e.g., Serrano* v. *Priest*, 5 Cal.3d 607, 616, 96 Cal. Rptr. 601, 624, 487 P.2d 1241, 1264 (1971) and authorities cited.

154. 385 U.S. 589 (1967).

155. *Id.* at 610.

156. *Id.* at 605-610. *See also Elfbrandt* v. *Russell*, 384 U.S. 11 (1966); *Murray* v. *Jamison*, 333 F.Supp. 1379 (W.D. N.C. 1971) (where neither work of municipal employee as switchboard operator in building-inspection department nor work of his department as a whole was adversely affected, his discharge for Klan membership was unconstitutional).

157. *Karst* v. *Regents of the University of California*, 2 Civil No. 38410 (Cal. Ct. App. Jan. 26, 1972), *aff'g* No. 962388 (Super. Ct. Los Angeles County October 21 and 24, 1969), 4 College Law Bull. 47 (1972).

158. R. MacIver, *Academic Freedom in Our Time* 153-54 (1955).

159. *Bruns* v. *Pomerleau*, 319 F.Supp. 58 (D. Md. 1970).

160. *Id.* at 64.
161. *Id.* at 69.
162. *NAACP* v. *Alabama,* 357 U.S. 449, 462 (1958); *Gibson* v. *Florida Legislative Comm'n,* 372 U.S. 539 (1963).
163. *NAACP* v. *Alabama,* 357 U.S. 449 (1958); *Gibson* v. *Florida Legislative Comm'n,* 372 U.S. 539 (1963).
164. 364 U.S. 479 (1960).
165. *Id.* at 490.
166. *Barenblatt* v. *United States,* 360 U.S. 109, 127 (1959).
167. 360 U.S. 109 (1959).
168. *Id.* at 112.
169. H. Beale, *A History of Freedom of Teaching in American Schools* 60 (1941).
170. H. Beale, *Are American Teachers Free?* 65 (1936).
171. *State* v. *Lundquist,* 262 Md. 534, 537, 278 A.2d 263, 265 (1971).
172. *Ibid.*
173. *Cramp* v. *Board of Public Instruction,* 368 U.S. 278 (1961).
174. *Stewart* v. *Washington,* 301 F.Supp. 610 (D. D.C. 1969).
175. *Haskett* v. *Washington,* 294 F.Supp. 912 (D. D.C. 1968).
176. *Wieman* v. *Updegraff,* 344 U.S. 183 (1952). *See also Haining* v. *Roberts,* 320 F.Supp. 1054 (S.D. Miss. 1970), *appeal dismissed,* 453 F.2d 1223 (5th Cir. 1971).
177. *Whitehall* v. *Elkins,* 389 U.S. 54 (1967).
178. *Baggett* v. *Bullitt,* 377 U.S. 360 (1964). *See also MacKay* v. *Rafferty,* 321 F.Supp. 1177 (N.D. Cal. 1970), *aff'd,* 400 U.S. 954 (1971).
179. *Georgia Conference of AAUP* v. *Board of Regents,* 246 F.Supp. 553, 554 (N.D. Ga. 1965).
180. *Ohlson* v. *Phillips,* 304 F.Supp. 1152, 1153 (D. Colo. 1969), *aff'd,* 397 U.S. 317 (1970). *See also Hosack* v. *Smiley,* 276 F.Supp. 876 (D. Colo. 1967), *aff'd per curiam,* 390 U.S. 744 (1968); *Knight* v. *Board of Regents,* 269 F.Supp. 339 (S.D. N.Y. 1967), *aff'd,* 390 U.S. 36 (1968); *Biklen* v. *Board of Educ.,* 333 F.Supp. 902 (N.D. N.Y. 1971).
181. *Cole* v. *Richardson,* 40 U.S.L.W. 4381 (U.S. April 18, 1972).
182. *National Ass'n of Letter Carriers* v. *Blount,* 305 F.Supp. 546 (D. D.C. 1969), *appeal dismissed,* 400 U.S. 801 (1971).
183. *Hanover* v. *Northrup,* 325 F.Supp. 170, 171 (D. Conn. 1970).

184. *Id.* at 172.
185. *Id.* at 173.
186. *Superintendent of Schools* v. *Jacobs,* Report of Bethuel L. Webster as Trial Examiner, p. 11 (1968), cited favorably in *Frain* v. *Baron,* 307 F.Supp. 27, 32 (E.D.N.Y. 1969). *See also West Virginia State Board of Education* v. *Barnette,* 319 U.S. 624 (1943).
187. *Frain* v. *Baron,* 307 F.Supp. 27, 32 (E.D.N.Y. 1969).
188. *State* v. *Lundquist,* 262 Md. 534, 278 A.2d 263 (1971).

IV. Freedom of Religion

At least in areas outside of our large cities, a teacher of an unorthodox faith traditionally has found it difficult to obtain a position. Writing in 1936, Beale found that "[o]utside of great cities it is universally difficult to place a Jew,"[1] and "[o]utside of large Northern cities a Catholic layman finds it extremely difficult to obtain an appointment."[2] Half of the schools outside of the Northeast or large cities would not employ Mormons, and Gentiles, it was reported, were discriminated against in Utah.[3] Only in the Northeast and in cities above one hundred thousand in population did an agnostic have a good change of appointment and atheists were even more unwelcome.[4] It is a fair assumption that while these attitudes have been ameliorated, they have not entirely disappeared as barriers to a teacher's employment in some areas.

A teacher who *is* employed in a community in which his religious convictions place him in a minority may be confronted with demands to inculcate his students with some form of religious ideology compatible with the majority faith. Although sectarianism was generally forbidden in the schools by World War I, *nonsectarian* exercises subsequently were required in many public schools.[5] In some communities such practices are either required or permitted today, even after Supreme Court decisions holding the practices unconstitutional. These "nonsectarian" exercises may conflict with the teacher's own convictions if the teacher is Jewish or agnostic and believes that he is being

105

required to teach Christianity. A teacher may also have religious scruples against participation in other school exercises, such as saluting the flag, or organizing Christmas parties or plays.

(1.) Can a state or a school system condition the employment of a teacher on his religious affiliation?

No. Neither public office nor public employment may be conditioned upon religious affiliation or belief. Nor may a government job be conditioned upon abandonment of religious practices that do not interfere with the obligations of the position. As the Supreme Court has said, Congress may not "enact a regulation providing that no . . . Jew . . . shall be appointed to federal office, or that no federal employee shall attend Mass or take any active part in missionary work."[6] States and school authorities are subject to similar prohibitions under the Fourteenth Amendment.

(2.) Do these principles apply to agnostics and atheists?

Yes. The Supreme Court has struck down, as a violation of the freedom of belief and religion guarantees of the First and Fourteenth Amendments, a Maryland requirement that a notary public declare his belief in the existence of God.[7]

(3.) Does a teacher have a constitutional right to refuse to participate in school functions or exercises which are incompatible with his religious beliefs?

This question has not been squarely decided. It seems clear, however, that if, as the courts have held, a teacher cannot be required to compromise his intellectual or moral convictions by leading his class in the pledge of allegiance,[8] he could not be required to salute the flag if this violated his religious scruples. The Supreme Court has expressly held that *students* who were Jehovah's Witnesses, and whose religious beliefs barred paying homage to symbols, had a constitutional right protected by the First Amendment to refrain from saluting the flag.[9]

Officially sanctioned Bible reading and prayer in the

public schools have been declared unconstitutional by the Supreme Court[10] in suits by parents and children. No question was raised in these cases regarding the constitutional right of *teachers* in such schools to refuse to take part in such programs on the ground that the programs violated their religious convictions, although such a challenge might well have had merit.

NOTES

1. H. Beale, *Are American Teachers Free?* 497 (1936).
2. *Id.* at 511.
3. *Id.* at 514.
4. *Id.* at 515.
5. *Id.* at 209, 211.
6. *United Public Workers* v. *Mitchell*, 330 U.S. 75, 100 (1947).
7. *Torcaso* v. *Watkins*, 367 U.S. 488 (1961).
8. *E.g., Hanover* v. *Northrup*, 325 F.Supp. 170 (D. Conn. 1970).
9. *West Virginia State Board of Educ.* v. *Barnette*, 319 U.S. 624 (1943).
10. *Engel* v. *Vitale*, 370 U.S. 421 (1962). *Abington School District* v. *Schempp*, 374 U.S. 203 (1963).

V. Freedom in Private Life

Although doctors and lawyers are subject to strict professional standards, generally they are not purged from their professions or deprived of their employment for private vices which have no demonstrable relationship to their fitness to practice. For example, gambling, temper and abusive language, and frequenting a disorderly house, have all been held not to be grounds for disbarment.[1]

In recent cases, courts, with one eye on the Constitution, have taken a similar approach with respect to the discharge of public employees. Thus, dismissal of a federal employee for "immoral" or "indecent" acts can be justified only if these acts "have some ascertainable deleterious effect on the efficiency of the service."[2] Rejecting "the notion that it could be an appropriate function of the federal bureaucracy to enforce the majority's conventional codes of conduct in the private lives of its employees," the court said that such an idea was "at war with elementary concepts of liberty, privacy, and diversity."[3]

More so than other public employees, teachers traditionally have been held to a standard of personal conduct that might have suffocated Caesar's wife. For example, until World War I, "[d]ancing, card-playing, smoking, drinking, theatre-going, and Sabbath-breaking were still regarded by multitudes as sinful. . . . The teacher was expected in all these matters to be exemplary."[4]

Thus, in 1883, Josiah Royce wrote that a teacher "may find of a sudden that his non-attendance at church, or the fact that he drinks beer with his lunch, or rides a bicycle, is considered of more moment than his power to instruct."[5] Even before he got into difficulties over evolution, John Scopes was criticized in Dayton for cigarette smoking and dancing.[6]

At one time under a contract used in a North Carolina town, teachers promised "not to go out with any young men except insofar as it may be necessary to stimulate Sunday School work"; "not to fall in love . . ."; "to remain in the dormitory or on the school grounds when not actively engaged in school or church work elsewhere"; and "to sleep at least eight hours each night. . . ."[7] In another contract signed in 1915, teachers promised, among other things, "not to keep company with men; to be home between the hours of 8:00 P.M. and 6:00 A.M. unless in attendance at a school function"; "not to loiter downtown in ice cream stores"; not to leave town at any time without permission of the chairman of the board, and not to get in a carriage or automobile with any man except her father or brother.[8]

Similar restraints were imposed even after the First World War. For example, a Virginia contract signed in 1935 specified that teachers could not keep company with "sorry young men." A Tennessee contract stipulated that "said teacher is to refrain from any and all questionable pastimes." An Alabama contract asked: "Do you promise that if employed, you will not have company or go automobile riding on Monday, Tuesday, Wednesday and Thursday nights?"[9] One young teacher echoed Royce's remark: "How I conduct my classes seems to be of no great interest to the school authorities, but what I do when school is not in session concerns them tremendously."[10]

Until recently the courts have not afforded much solace to teachers burdened by such restrictions.[11] Judicial attitudes towards efforts by school authorities to control a teacher's private life, however, are beginning to change in suits attacking the constitutionality of such practices.

(1.) Is a teacher constitutionally protected from adverse action by school authorities because they disapprove of the way he lives his private life?

Probably. The courts have been increasingly reluctant to uphold such penalties unless the State or the school authorities can show that the teacher's conduct has impaired his fitness to teach. Based on a growing judicial awareness that the Constitution limits the extent to which a state can control private conduct as a condition of public employment, these cases narrowly interpret statutory language authorizing a penalty to be imposed for "immorality," "unprofessional conduct" and the like, to exclude the conduct in question. For example:

(a.) An Ohio court held that a teacher could not be dismissed for "immorality" merely because he had used offensive language in a confidential letter to a former student. The court held that a teacher's private conduct is a proper concern to his employers "only to the extent it mars him as a teacher. . . . Where his professional achievement is unaffected, where the school community is placed in no jeopardy, his private acts are his own business and may not be the basis of discipline." It made no difference, the court ruled, that the teacher's reputation had been impaired by publication of his letter in the local newspaper through someone else's indiscretion.[12] Although the decision turned on an interpretation of the Ohio statute, the court indicated that the teacher's letters were protected by provisions of the United States Constitution conferring rights of free speech and privacy.

(b.) The California Supreme Court ruled that under California statutes authorizing revocation of a teaching certificate for immoral and unprofessional conduct and acts involving moral turpitude, a teacher's certificate could not be revoked because of his participation in a homosexual relationship with another teacher absent a showing that the relationship affected his fitness to teach. The court agreed with the teacher's constitutional argument that "[n]o person can be denied government employment because of factors unconnected with the responsibilities of that employ-

ment,"[13] and concluded that "[t]he power of the state to
regulate professions and conditions of government employment must not arbitrarily impair the right of the individual
to live his private life, apart from his job, as he deems
fit."[14] The court also observed that "an unqualified proscription against immoral conduct would raise serious constitutional problems" involving the teacher's right of privacy.[15]
The court avoided these constitutional problems by narrowly construing the California statutes.

(c.) One court held that the termination of a postal
clerk's employment because he had been living with a
woman to whom he was not married was arbitrary and
capricious and violated his right to due process, as well as
"his right to privacy as guaranteed by the 9th Amendment"
to the United States Constitution.[16] Although a teacher
occupies a more sensitive position, another court has
stated: "Surely incidents of extramarital heterosexual conduct against a background of years of satisfactory teaching
would not constitute 'immoral conduct' [under the relevant
state statute] sufficient to justify revocation of a life
diploma without any showing of an adverse effect on fitness
to teach."[17] The court's opinion showed an awareness of
the constitutional issues which would be raised by a contrary interpretation of the state law.

That a teacher's private conduct, standing alone, cannot constitutionally be made the business of the State is
reflected by the decision in a recent Texas case. A teacher-
athletic coach in a rural school district was dismissed for
"failure to meet accepted moral standards of conduct for
the teaching profession" because of his association with a
waitress in town. The dismissal occurred following a report
by a board member that after a basketball game, at around
midnight, the teacher and the waitress had driven together
to a country road and parked, and that the board member
had observed them together in the car for about 30
minutes. The court ordered the teacher reinstated with
back pay and awarded him attorneys' fees. Noting the
teacher's claim that he was discharged for exercising First
Amendment rights, the court said:

School districts may examine the conduct of teachers both in and out of the classrooms. . . . Nevertheless, before a teacher can possibly be discharged for personal conduct, the court feels that a showing must be made that such conduct had a direct effect on the teacher's success in performing classroom duties. There was no evidence in this case that [the teacher's] relationship with Mrs. Bumpass interfered with his teaching duties in any way. Without this showing the discharge is impermissible.[18]

It is an open question when, if ever, a teacher constitutionally could be disciplined merely because his violation of important and generally accepted community values has become so notorious as to impair his ability to command the respect and confidence of his students or fellow teachers.[19] A court upheld a state university's withdrawal of the plaintiff's appointment as a librarian where he sought to marry another man and applied for a marriage license with his prospective male spouse—an event that received the attention of the local news and television media. Refusing to categorize the Board of Regents' action as arbitrary, unreasonable or capricious, the court stressed that it was not confronted with "a case involving mere homosexual propensities on the part of a prospective employee" or "a case in which an applicant is excluded from employment because of a desire clandestinely to pursue homosexual conduct."[20]

(2.) Can a teacher constitutionally be disciplined or his employment terminated because of a private associational relationship disapproved by the community?

No, at least absent a showing that the relationship has substantially impaired his usefulness as a teacher. This is the teaching of the *Morrison* case, where to avoid constitutional problems the California Supreme Court held that the California statutes did not authorize revocation of a teaching certificate on the ground that the teacher had engaged in a private homosexual relationship.[21]

In a more recent case a black police officer alleged that

his employment was terminated because he allowed two white women employed on an antipoverty project to board in his home with his family. His employer expressed concern "with the public's response to women of the white race staying at the home of a black police officer with his family." In the view of the defendant city officials, city personnel had to "stay in the middle of the road" because of racial tensions resulting from school desegregation and other matters. The federal district court entered summary judgment for the defendants. Reversing the district court, the United States Court of Appeals concluded that a private citizen would have a constitutional right to engage in the activity in question, and that if the police officer demonstrated that he was discharged or forced to resign as a result of such activity, the burden would then rest on the defendants to show that his conduct "would materially and substantially impair his usefulness as a police officer."[22]

(3.) Can a teacher constitutionally be required to live within the boundaries of his employing jurisdiction?

The answer is not yet clear and may depend on the facts of the particular case.

In a recent case brought by a schoolteacher, the Supreme Court of New Hampshire struck down, as a violation of both the Federal and State Constitutions, a city ordinance requiring that all classified employees of the city including schoolteachers, absent a special permit, be or become within twelve months of their employment residents of the city. The court ruled that "[t]he right of every citizen to live where he chooses and to travel freely not only within the state but across its borders is a fundamental right which is guaranteed both by our own and the Federal Constitutions," and that the ordinance restricted these fundamental rights. On the record made in the case, the court held, there was no justification for denying schoolteachers the right to live where they wished, even if such a restriction might be warranted with respect to some categories of public employees.[23] The court rejected the city's argument that those who are employed by the city should help support the cost of their employment by contributing to the economy of the city and its tax base.

The Supreme Court of Wyoming, on the other hand, found no merit in the contention that a school board acted unconstitutionally in denying continued employment to teachers for alleged violations of a board rule stipulating that "[n]ew teachers . . . will be expected to reside in the community at least five days a week. . . ." The court relied in part on the fact that the board had provided teacherages at a minimal rental where the teachers could be housed, and the fact that the teachers had voluntarily contracted to abide by the rule.[24]

A Michigan court upheld a school district policy requiring professional personnel holding *administrative* positions to reside within the school district, ruling that "[i]f the question of the beneficial effect of a residence requirement for public employees on public employment services is reasonably debatable, substantive due process is not violated. . . ."[25] The court found that question, on the record presented, "reasonably debatable."

NOTES

1. Note, *Disbarment: Non-Professional Conduct Demonstrating Unfitness to Practice,* 43 Cornell L.Q. 489, 493 (1958). *See* discussion in *Morrison* v. *State Board of Educ.,* 1 Cal. 3d 214, 221-22, 82 Cal. Rptr. 175, 179-81, 461 P.2d 375, 379-81 (1969).

2. *Norton* v. *Macy,* 417 F.2d 1161, 1165 (D.C. Cir. 1969).

3. *Ibid.* at 1165. *See also Mindel* v. *U.S. Civil Service Comm'n,* 312 F.Supp. 485 (N.D. Cal. 1970).

4. H. Beale, *A History of Freedom of Teaching in American Schools* 170-71 (1941).

5. Royce, *The Freedom of Teaching,* Overland Monthly, 235, 239 (1883).

6. L. Allen, *Bryan and Darrow at Dayton* 109 (1925).

7. Ewing, *Blue Laws for School Teachers,* 156 Harpers Magazine 329-38 (1928).

8. New York State *Education,* May 1971, p. 32.

9. Cooke, *Blue Law Blues*, The Nation's Schools, October 1935, p. 33.

10. *Id.* at 32.

11. *See e.g., Gover* v. *Stovall*, 237 Ky. App. 172, 176-78, 35 S.W.2d 24, 25-26 (1931); *Horosko* v. *School District*, 335 Pa. 369, 6 A.2d 866 (1939), *cert. denied*, 308 U.S. 553 (1939). *See Goldsmith* v. *Board of Educ.*, 66 Cal. App. 157, 225 P. 783 (1924).

12. *Jarvella* v. *Willoughby-Eastlake City School District Board of Educ.*, 12 Ohio Misc. 288, 291, 41 Ohio Op. 2d 423, 425, 233 N.E.2d 143, 146 (1967).

13. *Morrison* v. *State Board of Educ.*, 1 Cal.3d 214, 234, 82 Cal. Rptr. 175, 191, 461 P.2d 375, 391 (1969). *See also Norton* v. *Macy*, 417 F.2d 1161, 1167 (D.C. Cir. 1969).

14. 1 Cal.3d at 239, 82 Cal. Rptr. at 194, 461 P.2d at 394.

15. 1 Cal.3d at 233, 82 Cal Rptr. at 190, 461 P.2d at 390.

16. *Mindel* v. *U.S. Civil Service Comm'n*, 312 F.Supp. 485 (N.D. Cal. 1970). *See also Williams* v. *United States*, 434 F.2d 1346, 1355-56 (Ct. Cl. 1970) (Nichols J., concurring). *Cf. Carter* v. *United States*, 407 F.2d 1238 (D.C. Cir. 1968).

17. *Morrison* v. *State Board of Educ.*, 1 Cal.3d 214, 225-26, 82 Cal. Rptr. 175, 183, 461 P.2d 375, 383 (1969). *Cf. Schreiber* v. *Joint School District No. 1*, 335 F.Supp. 745, 748 n.2 (E.D. Wis. 1972) (teacher dismissed because she had lived in her fiance's home prior to marriage: "No opinion is expressed as to whether or not the issue of right to privacy is involved here and, if it is, if the state's interest here compelled such interference with plaintiff's personal life").

18. *Caddell* v. *Johnson*, Civil Action No. CA-7-615 (N.D. Tex. June 30, 1972).

19. *See Morrison* v. *State Board of Educ.* 1 Cal.3d 214, 229-30, 82 Cal. Rptr. 175, 186-87, 461 P.2d 375, 386-87 (1969). *Cf. Mindel* v. *U.S. Civil Service Comm'n*, 312 F.Supp. 485, 487 (N.D. Cal. 1970); *Carter* v. *United States*, 407 F.2d 1238, 1245-46 (D.C. Cir. 1968); *McConnell* v. *Anderson*, 451 F.2d 193, 196 (8th Cir. 1971), *cert. denied*, 40 U.S.L.W. 3484 (U.S. Apr. 3, 1972); *Langford* v. *City of Texarkana*, 337 F.Supp. 723, 728 (W.D. Ark. 1972); *Stewart* v. *East Baton Rouge Parish School Board*, 251 So.2d 487, 491 (Ct. App. La. 1971).

20. *McConnell* v. *Anderson*, 451 F.2d 193, 196 (8th Cir. 1971).

21. *Morrison* v. *State Board of Educ.*, 1 Cal.3d 214, 82 Cal. Rptr. 175, 461 P.2d 375 (1969).
22. *Battle* v. *Mulholland*, 439 F.2d 321, 323-25 (5th Cir. 1971). *Cf. Bruns* v. *Pomerleau*, 319 F.Supp. 58 (D. Md. 1970). *Compare Langford* v. *City of Texarkana*, 337 F.Supp. 723, 728 (W.D. Ark. 1972).
23. *Donnelly* v. *City of Manchester*, 274 A.2d 789, 791 (N.H. 1971).
24. *O'Melia* v. *Sweetwater County School District No. 1*, No. 4046 (Wyo. May 25, 1972).
25. *Park* v. *Lansing School District*, 32 Mich. App. 752, 755, 189 N.W.2d 60, 61 (1971). *Cf. Williams* v. *Civil Service Comm'n*, 383 Mich. 507, 514-15, 176 N.W.2d 593, 596-97 (1970); *In re City of Warren, Mich. and Warren Firefighters Ass'n*, Local 1383, 57 Lab. Arb. 585, 590-92 (1971).

VI. Freedom to Select Mode of Dress And Grooming

In 1915, one teaching contract obligated a female teacher not to dress in bright colors, not to dye her hair, to wear at least two petticoats, and not to wear dresses more than two inches above the ankle.[1] In 1924 Santa Paula, California forbade bobbed hair and dismissed one teacher solely because she bobbed hers. Sleeveless dresses, sheer stockings, and cosmetics have been banned or disapproved in their turn. In a West Virginia town, women teachers were required in 1928 to fasten their galoshes up all the way.[2] Some school authorities still attempt to control a teacher's mode of dress or grooming, although today the battleground has changed, and the restriction is more likely to be one which forbids a teacher to wear a dress more than two inches above the knee.[3]

Nor are females the only faculty members whose personal appearance school officials have sought to control. For example, although Samson had flowing locks, Aristotle, Plato, Jesus, Moses and Lincoln wore beards, and even Uncle Sam sports a goatee,[4] official disapproval and discipline of male teachers who seek to follow in their footsteps is not uncommon.

(1.) Can school officials constitutionally discipline or terminate the employment of a teacher because he does not conform to conventional standards of grooming?

No. Efforts by school authorities to regulate the personal appearance of teachers and students increasingly have been challenged in court, on a number of theories. It is alleged that such regulation unconstitutionally (1) infringes upon "symbolic speech" in violation of the First and Fourteenth Amendments; (2) interferes with personal "liberty" secured by the due process clause of the Fourteenth Amendment; (3) intrudes upon a right of privacy—the right to be let alone—which, it is contended, is secured by the "penumbra" of the First or Ninth Amendment; and (4) denies equal protection of the laws secured by the Fourteenth Amendment.

Although there is conflict in the student cases[5]—a conflict as yet unresolved by the Supreme Court—the decisions generally have sustained constitutional challenges by teachers to rules or decrees purporting to control their personal appearance.

(a.) A California state court held that a school board cannot remove a teacher from regular classroom duties because he insists on wearing a beard, absent a showing that the beard is untidy or unkempt, or has an adverse effect on the educational process or on the behavior of students. The court held that the wearing of a beard is "symbolic speech"—an expression of personality—protected by the First and Fourteenth Amendments.[6]

(b.) The acting commissioner of the New York State Department of Education ordered the reinstatement of a probationary teacher who had been suspended for failing to trim his hair and mustache to the specifications of the school board. Absent proof that the teacher's appearance was bizarre or disruptive, or diminished his teaching effectiveness, the acting commissioner ruled, the school board could not, "consistent with our basic constitutional framework," impose what it deemed to be "the standards of appearance of the community" as a condition of employment.[7]

(c.) A Florida court ruled that a school board could not constitutionally deny reappointment to a black teacher for refusing to comply with his principal's request that he remove his goatee. The court held that the wearing of the goatee was constitutionally protected liberty under the due process clause of the Fourteenth Amendment and was also entitled to First Amendment protection because it was worn as "an appropriate expression of his heritage, culture and racial pride as a black man." The court concluded that the principal's request was "arbitrary, unreasonable, and based on personal preference," and that the decision to refuse reappointment was "not free from institutional racism."[8]

(d.) An Alabama federal court held that a principal's rule against male teachers wearing mustaches was "arbitrary, unreasonable, and capricious" and violated the due process clause of the Fourteenth Amendment. In a suit by a teacher terminated for disobeying the rule, the court condemned the regulation as "a gross example of a rule based upon personal taste of an administrative official which is not a permissible base upon which to build rules for the organization of a public institution."[9]

(e.) The Rhode Island Commissioner of Education invalidated a school committee's decision not to renew a teacher's contract and to deny him tenure because of his refusal to trim his mustache or cut his hair when requested to do so by the chairman of the school committee. Holding the school committee's action violative of the Fourteenth Amendment, the commissioner ruled that "the burden of proving that . . . [the teacher's] appearance was detrimental to his teaching rests upon the school committee," and that no such showing had been made.[10]

(2.) To what extent can school authorities constitutionally control a teacher's mode of dress?

It would appear that, at the least, any effort by a school system to regulate a teacher's mode of dress must be based upon factual conditions warranting the conclusion that the forbidden attire would disrupt the educational process.

In one recent case a female physical-education teacher

was observed by the superintendent of schools and the high-school principal giving swimming instruction to a class of junior-high school boys while attired in a two-piece "bikini-type" bathing suit. She was directed to refrain from wearing the suit while giving swimming instruction in the schools. She contended that this directive "impinged upon her individual freedom." Ruling for the teacher, the New York Commissioner of Education held:

> There is no question but that a board of education, as any employer, may establish reasonable standards with respect to the general mode of attire of its employees in connection with their various work assignments. However, respondent in this case has not sought to establish such standards, but rather has based its action on the contention that petitioner's bathing suit was a "distracting and disruptive influence."
>
> The record before me contains no proof in support of that contention. To the contrary, the director of athletics of respondent's schools indicates that the discipline in petitioner's classes has always been excellent. Respondent does not contend that petitioner's attire was indecent, and has not established that it was disruptive of the educational process. Absent such proof, the appeal must be sustained.[11]

In another case an arbitrator, discussing but not reaching the constitutional issue, held that a school superintendent's directive to all female teachers proscribing the wearing of pant suits on pain of being sent home for the day without pay violated a collective agreement authorizing the administration to promulgate "reasonable" personnel rules, since the directive had no bona-fide relationship to the educational process. The evidence indicated that pant suits were permitted in many school districts in the state. The facts also showed that in the lower grades pant suits are an aid in teaching since, for example, a teacher in these grades must stoop down or over to be near to and identify with her students, raise her arm to write on the blackboard, and engage in elementary physical endeavors in the classroom and the gymnasium.[12]

NOTES

1. New York State *Education*, May 1971, p. 32.
2. H. Beale, *Are American Teachers Free?* 390-91 (1936).
3. *Tourtelotte* v. *Vinita Board of Educ.*, No. 69-C-227 (N.D. Okla. Aug. 13, 1970).
4. *See In the Matter of the Arbitration between Local 100, Transport Workers Union of America and Manhattan and Bronx Surface Transit Operating Authority* (Nov. 11, 1969, T. Kheel) (quoting from the November, 1969 issue of Penthouse Magazine); *Richards* v. *Thurston*, 304 F.Supp. 449, 451 (D. Mass. 1969), *aff'd*, 424 F.2d 1281 (1st Cir. 1970).
5. *See, e.g.*, cases collected in *Richards* v. *Thurston*, 424 F.2d 1281, 1282 n.3 (1st Cir. 1970).
6. *Finot* v. *Pasadena City Board of Educ.*, 250 Cal. App. 2d 189, 58 Cal. Rptr. 520 (1968).
7. *In the Matter of John Collins*, No. 8051 (N.Y. Commissioner of Educ. Aug. 26, 1969), GERR No. 313, B-11, Sept. 8, 1969.
8. *Braxton* v. *Board of Public Instruction*, 303 F.Supp. 958, 959 (M.D. Fla. 1969).
9. *Ramsey* v. *Hopkins*, 320 F.Supp. 477, 482 (N.D. Ala. 1970), *rev'd on other grounds*, 447 F.2d 128 (5th Cir. 1971). *Cf. In re City and County of San Francisco*, 55 Lab. Arb. 970, 975 (1970).
10. *Marchand* v. *School Committee* (R.I. Commissioner of Educ. Oct. 26, 1971). *But see Farmer* v. *Catmull*, 339 F.Supp. 70 (D. Utah 1972) (work regulation of city streets department, stating "[h]air may be worn full, but in no event to hang over ears or collars," upheld over constitutional objection).
11. *In the Matter of Heather Martin*, No. 8156 (N. Y. Commissioner of Educ. Aug. 3, 1971).
12. *In re School District of Kingsley and Kingsley Educ. Ass'n*, 56 Lab. Arb. 1138 (1971).

VII. Freedom From Arbitrary or Discriminatory Action by School Officials

School authorities may act unconstitutionally even where they are not engaging in reprisals for the exercise of constitutional rights. They are forbidden by the equal protection clause of the Fourteenth Amendment to make invidious and unjustified distinctions between teachers on the basis of race or other unreasonable criteria. Arbitrary or capricious action by school officials, moreover, may violate the due process clause of the Fourteenth Amendment.

The guiding principles have been set forth by the Supreme Court. In *Wieman* v. *Updegraff*,[1] the Court said: "We need not pause to consider whether an abstract right to public employment exists. It is sufficient to say that constitutional protection does extend to the public servant whose exclusion pursuant to a statute is patently arbitrary or discriminatory." Later, in *Slochower* v. *Board of Education*,[2] the Court observed: "To state that a person does not have a constitutional right to government employment is only to say that he must comply with *reasonable*, lawful, and *nondiscriminatory* terms laid down by the proper authorities." These principles apply to refusals to hire or promote a teacher, as well as to terminations and disciplinary actions.[3]

(1.) Must a school board be "colorblind" in making personnel decisions?

Not necessarily. The race of a teacher may be taken into account in personnel decisions where the objective is a worthy one. For example, in one case the Newark school board abolished a promotional list, required under a contract with a teachers' association, which had been developed on the basis of oral and written examinations for anyone wishing to be a principal or vice-principal. The superintendent then recommended appointments to such posts with the objective of obtaining administrators sensitive to the problems of educating a predominantly black student population, taking color into account. The actions of the board and superintendent were held not to violate the constitutional rights of white teachers on the promotional list.[4]

Similarly, race may be taken into account where the objective is to cure the effects of past racial discrimination. Indeed, several courts have required school boards, upon proof of racial discrimination against black teachers, to hire black teaching applicants so as to achieve a particular racial ratio among the faculty.[5] In the South, where special rules have been formulated by the courts in an effort to protect black teachers and principals against displacement incident to school desegregation, the decree which most federal trial courts have been directed to enter provides that where a staff reduction results in a dismissal or demotion, "no staff vacancy may be filled through recruitment of a person of a race, color, or national origin different from that of the individual dismissed or demoted, until each displaced staff member who is qualified has had an opportunity to fill the vacancy and has failed to accept an offer to do so."[6]

(2.) Can racial discrimination be proved by showing the racial effect of a school board policy, or must a racially discriminatory purpose be shown?

Where a school board policy or a state law has the effect of substantially and disproportionately disadvantaging a minority group, "it must be justified by an overriding purpose independent of its racial effects" in order to withstand an equal protection attack.[7] In a recent case a Mississippi school system initiated a policy that required teachers hired for the first time during the 1969–70 school year, and all future teacher applicants, to achieve a combined score of 1,000 on the National Teachers Examination as a condition of employment. The rule substantially disadvantaged black teachers. Applying the "overriding purpose" standard and striking down the rule, the United States Court of Appeals for the Fifth Circuit stated: "Whenever the effect of a law or policy produces such a racial distortion it is subject to strict scrutiny. . . . Even though this policy does not on its face purport to classify along racial lines . . . its effects can be just as devastating."[8]

The court acknowledged that where a test has a "valid function" in an effort to improve the faculty, "and is fairly applied to all teachers, it outweighs the fact that it may result in excluding more blacks than whites."[9] But the court pointed out that the NTE cut-off score requirement had been set by the defendants without any investigation or study of the validity and reliability of the examination or the cut-off score as a means of selecting teachers for hiring or re-employment, and without consultation with the Educational Testing Service. It was established, moreover, that the NTE measured "only a fraction of the characteristics required for effective classroom performance. It does not measure manual skills, teaching aptitude, attitudes, personal characteristics or classroom teaching performance."[10] And the proof showed that the defendants' purpose in instituting the policy, far from being "independent of invidious racial discrimination," was in fact to discriminate against black teachers.[11] In these circumstances, the court held that the policy violated the equal protection clause.

(3.) What are some examples of invidious discrimination by school officials against a teacher, other than racial discrimination, which are forbidden by the Constitution?

A school system could not constitutionally discriminate against a teacher because of his religion.[12] Such discrimination would violate the equal protection clause in addition to the clause of the First Amendment, made applicable to the

FREEDOM FROM ACTION 125

states by the Fourteenth Amendment, protecting the "free exercise" of religion against infringement by government.

It is also clear that school officials are barred by the Constitution from discriminating against a teacher because of his ancestry or national origin.[13]

(4.) Can a state or school authorities constitutionally favor teachers who are citizens over those who are aliens?

No. Such discrimination would violate the equal protection clause. The Supreme Court has ruled that alien welfare applicants are denied equal protection by statutes conditioning welfare eligibility upon citizenship or residence in the United States for a specified number of years.[14] Relying upon this decision, a federal district court held that the refusal of a city junior college to grant tenure to two teachers because of their alienage violated the equal protection clause. The court rejected the justification tendered by the defendants that the state has an interest in providing its own citizens with work, and that if aliens were given tenure, nontenured employees with citizenship would be laid off before tenured aliens in the event of an economic slowdown. Another attempted justification—that the allegiance of aliens to the principles of the United States remained questionable—was rejected as an effort to impose an additional burden upon aliens not contemplated by the Immigration and Nationality Act, which makes suitable provision for excluding those with questionable allegiance.[15]

(5.) Can school officials constitutionally discriminate against a teacher on the basis of sex?

Not unless they can show, at the very least, that the sex-based discrimination is reasonable, not arbitrary, and is rationally related to a legitimate goal of the school system.[16] Some courts have suggested that because a basic right to work or pursue a profession free of invidious discrimination is at stake in such cases, or because sex is a "suspect classification," the school authorities must meet a more stringent test and show that the discrimination promotes a "compelling governmental interest."[17]

It seems clear that certain types of discrimination by school authorities on the basis of sex could satisfy neither test. It is patently unreasonable, for example, to pay women less than men where they are equally well qualified and do the same work, or to discriminate against women in affording opportunities for promotion. Less overt and more subtle policies serving to confine women to positions of lower pay or responsibility in the educational system may also be unconstitutional.[18] It may not be entirely irrational, on the other hand, for a school system to favor males in selecting a boys' wrestling coach.

Recently enacted amendments to Title VII of the Civil Rights Act of 1964, which forbids discrimination in employment on account of sex, have extended the protections of the Act to state and local government employees, including public school teachers.[19] Title VII provides, in what has come to be known as the "BFOQ exception," that it shall not be an unlawful employment practice for an employer "to hire and employ employees . . . on the basis of [their] 'sex' in those certain instances where . . . sex . . . is a bona fide occupational qualification reasonably necessary to the normal operation of that particular business or enterprise . . ."[20]

The Equal Employment Opportunity Commission, an administrative agency established by Title VII and given power, with respect to discrimination in public employment, to investigate and conciliate charges,[21] has issued guidelines interpreting the Act, including the BFOQ exception.[22] These guidelines, which are entitled to "great deference" by the courts,[23] shed light upon types of sex-based discrimination by school authorities which may be vulnerable under Title VII. While a violation of Title VII does not necessarily amount to a violation of the equal protection clause, it is probable that interpretations of Title VII by the EEOC and by the courts will have a significant bearing upon judicial resolution of the parallel constitutional issues.[24] A teacher who alleges discrimination on account of sex should, in addition to contacting her teacher organization, file a complaint promptly with the

chairman of the EEOC in Washington, after consultation
with counsel if possible.

(6.) What do the EEOC guidelines provide?

One section of the guidelines provides that the BFOQ
exception is not satisfied where the refusal to hire a woman
because of her sex is based on the preferences of co-
workers, on assumptions of the comparative employment
characteristics of women in general (for example, the
assumption that the turnover rate among women is higher
than among men), or on "stereotyped characterizations
of the sexes." Individuals must be "considered on the basis
of individual capacities and not on the basis of any
characteristics generally attributed to the group."[25]

The guidelines also state that it is an unlawful employment practice for an employer to discriminate between
men and women with regard to fringe benefits. Employment benefits available to employees and their families
which are conditioned on whether the employee is the
"head of the household" or "principle wage earner" in the
family unit—benefits which tend to be available only to
male employees and their families—constitute a prima
facie violation of the Act.[26]

Under the guidelines, moreover, it is an unlawful employment practice for an employer to (1) make available
benefits for the wives and families of male employees
where the same benefits are not made available to the
husbands and families of female employees; (2) make
available benefits for the wives of male employees which
are not made available to female employees, or (3) make
available benefits for the husbands of female employees
which are not made available to male employees. For
example, a school board could not give maternity benefits
for the wives of male teachers while withholding such
benefits from female teachers.[27] Nor, presumably, could
a board pay a dependency allowance to male teachers, but
deny the allowance to a female teacher putting her husband through college.

The guidelines also make it an unlawful employment
practice for an employer to have a pension or retirement

plan which establishes different optional or compulsory retirement ages based on sex, or which differentiates in benefits on the basis of sex.[28] A state law or school board policy specifying that male teachers may or must retire at age 65, but pegging the retirement age for female teachers at 62, would violate this provision. Similarly, a retirement plan provision under which female teachers receive lower annuities than male teachers on the theory that the life expectancy of women in general is longer than that of men also would appear to be invalid under the guidelines.

In an earlier era, many school boards limited the employment of married women.[29] Any remaining vestiges of such a policy are vulnerable under a section of the guidelines stating that "an employer's rule which forbids or restricts the employment of married women and which is not applicable to married men is a discrimination based on sex prohibited by Title VII of the Civil Rights Act."[30] Without expressing any opinion as to whether such a rule could be justified under any circumstances, the guidelines declare that "sex as a bona fide occupational qualification must be justified in terms of the peculiar requirements of the particular job and not on the basis of a general principle such as the desirability of spreading work."[31]

(7.) May school officials constitutionally require a pregnant teacher to resign or take a leave of absence without pay at a specified time before her delivery date?

The cases are in conflict, although most of the decisions have held such policies unconstitutional.[32]

An Ohio federal court, striking down a board policy requiring the mandatory resignation of pregnant employees after their fifth month of pregnancy, stated:

No persuasive evidence has been adduced which tends to support the Board's contention that . . . [its mandatory retirement policy] is either medically, psychologically or administratively justified. There is, in fact, evidence in the record which compels a conclusion contrary to the one urged upon this court by the defendant Board. It appears that the first trimester of pregnancy (months 1–3), and not the second months (4–6) are the most dangerous, in medical terms, to the expectant mother. Yet the Board does not require the pregnant teacher to resign at the outset of pregnancy, but rather, somewhat illogically, during the second trimester.[33]

The court declared that the board policy, to be valid, could not deal with women in stereotyped terms, but "must provide for a case-by-case determination of inability to perform teaching duties for reasons of pregnancy."[34] A divided state court in Pennsylvania, however, upheld a similar policy over two vigorous dissents, one based on federal constitutional grounds as well as state law.[35]

The courts are also divided on the constitutionality of board policies requiring teachers to take mandatory maternity leave—as distinguished from resigning—after a particular month of pregnancy. In a leading case, *Cohen v. Chesterfield County School Board*,[36] a Virginia federal court held that a school-board regulation requiring a teacher to take a leave of absence at the end of her fifth month of pregnancy discriminated against women in violation of the equal protection clause. The court held that no medical or psychological reason for the board's regulation had been shown by the defendants, and concluded that "since no two pregnancies are alike, decisions of when a pregnant teacher should discontinue working are matters best left up to the woman and her doctor."[37]

Nor, in the court's judgment, had the defendants advanced any tenable administrative justification for the regulation, since they had neither produced data to support their alleged fears that pregnant teachers would be pushed with resulting injury to the fetus and disabled from carrying out responsibilities in fire drills, nor conducted a substantial study upon which to base the contention that absences would increase during the latter stages of pregnancy. The court held that "[b]ecause pregnancy, though unique to women, is like other medical conditions, the failure to treat it as such amounts to discrimination which is without rational basis, and therefore is violative of the equal protection clause of the Fourteenth Amendment."[38]

A California federal court, in a preliminary ruling, went further and concluded that a board policy requiring a certificated employee to take maternity leave without pay after her *seventh* month of pregnancy violated the equal protection clause.[39] The court ruled that the policy neither promoted a compelling interest of the school authorities—a test the court held applicable[40]—nor was rationally related to a legitimate objective of the board. It was undisputed that the teacher challenging the policy was medically able to work efficiently until the date of her delivery if she chose to do so, and the defendants presented no proof that work during advanced pregnancy would be in any way harmful to her.[41] The court rejected the board's argument that permitting certificated females to work until the date of delivery would increase the school district's potential tort liability because of the increased likelihood of injury to those employees. This contention, the court stated, had "no basis in law or fact" since the employee would be bound to exercise that degree of care required of "a reasonable pregnant female situated such as she."[42]

In *LaFleur* v. *Cleveland Board of Education*,[43] however, a federal court rejected the claim that a board regulation requiring teachers to take a leave of absence without pay after their fourth month of pregnancy violated the equal protection clause.* The court found that the primary purpose of the rule was to maintain the continuity of the classroom program, and that the rule was reasonable in light of its purpose. The court also cited evidence that the incidence of violence in the Cleveland schools had been increasing; that there had been numerous assaults on teachers; and that many teachers had been accidentally injured as a result of falls in corridors and hallways, and

*As this book went to press, an appellate court reversed the decision in the *LaFleur* case, holding that the board's rule was arbitrary, unreasonable and lacking sufficient support in the medical evidence.

concluded that "[i]n an environment where the possibility of violence and accident exists, pregnancy greatly magnifies the probability of serious injury."[44] In addition, the evidence showed that prior to the adoption of the rule pregnant teachers had suffered "many indignities" and the school program had been interrupted by "children pointing, giggling, laughing, and making snide remarks."[45] The evidence further showed that although prior to the adoption of the policy no child had ever been born in the classroom, a few times it had been "very close."[46] The court also focused on evidence of physiological changes accompanying pregnancy that tend to weaken a female's health in certain respects.[47]

The *LaFleur* ruling has been criticized for its reliance on the need for classroom continuity.[48] This need, another court stated, "is indisputably frustrated when . . . a female teacher, otherwise qualified and capable of performing her duties, is hoicked out of the classroom for . . . [a sizeable portion] of the effective teaching year because she has become pregnant. The impact of such removal, particularly in the lower grades wherein children receive all their instruction from a single teacher, must be substantial indeed."[49] Another federal court distinguished the *LaFleur* case on its facts since it "rested in large measure on specific findings . . . that the high incidence of physical violence in the Cleveland public schools against teachers placed pregnant women teachers in some jeopardy."[50]

Recently, however, the U.S. Court of Appeals for the Fifth Circuit, by a divided vote, ruled that a Texas Employment Commission policy terminating the employment of pregnant female employees two months prior to the expected delivery date was consistent with the equal protection clause.[51] The majority relied in part upon evidence of the weakened condition of women during the latter stages of pregnancy, and expressed concern with the administrative problems facing the Commission were it required to treat each pregnant employee on a case-by-case basis.[52] The court posed these rhetorical questions:

Is it constitutionally required of a state agency or any other employer of many females that they shall make a daily, or even momentary, evaluation of the conditions and hazards of its pregnant female employees after they have reached the far advanced stage?

Is it conducive to the reasonably efficient operation of a state agency that it should involve itself in strife, discord, unhappiness, jealousies, and recriminations caused by allowing one woman to work through the eighth or ninth month of pregnancy as a matter of opinion on the part of some supervisor while requiring another to stop at the end of the seventh?[53]

Taking issue with this reasoning, the federal district court in the California case, relying upon a Supreme Court decision,[54] stated that a practice otherwise violative of the equal protection clause cannot be upheld merely because the alternative "might require more work on the part of the administering agency."[55] The court also distinguished the case of a State Employment Commission from that of a school district, in which the use of substitutes is a common and widespread practice.[56] Reviewing the relevant decisions, the California court stated that even if the defendant school district had attempted to support its maternity leave policy by referring to every rationale forwarded in any of the cases dealing with a similar issue, it remained true that its methods of dealing with pregnancy were "draconian" and that no matter what the objectives of the district were, they could be served by less restrictive means.[57]

(8.) What do the EEOC guidelines provide with respect to employment policies relating to pregnancy and childbirth?

The guidelines make it a prima facie violation of Title VII for an employer to exclude employees "from employment . . . because of pregnancy . . ."[58] The guidelines also require that "[d]isabilities caused by or contributed to by pregnancy, miscarriage, abortion, childbirth, and recovery therefrom are, for all job-related purposes, temporary disabilities and should be treated as such under any health or temporary disability insurance or sick leave plan available in connection with employment."[59] Moreover, "[w]ritten and unwritten employment policies and practices involving matters such as the commencement and duration of leave, the availability of extensions, and accrual of seniority and other benefits and privileges, reinstatement, and payment under any health or temporary disability insurance or sick leave plan . . . shall be applied to disability due to pregnancy and childbirth on the same terms and conditions as they are applied to other temporary disabilities."[60]

Thus, the guidelines require that if, in the case of other temporary disabilities, leave of absence commences only upon the employee's election or pursuant to medical necessity, or the leave is with pay until accumulated sick leave days have been exhausted, the same policy must be applied to temporary disabilities due to pregnancy and childbirth.*

(9.) Under the Constitution and the EEOC guidelines, can school authorities require a female teacher to wait a specified period of time following delivery before being eligible for reemployment?

The courts are divided on the constitutional issue. In *LaFleur*, the court upheld the constitutionality of a maternity leave provision under which female teachers were not eligible for reemployment until three months

---

*As this book went to press, an Illinois federal court issued a preliminary injunction restraining a school board from enforcing a mandatory maternity leave policy and enjoining the board to treat maternity leave in the same fashion as sick leave for purposes of sick pay, seniority and placement of returning teachers. *Bravo* v. *Board of Educ,* 4 FEP cases 994 (N.D. Ill. 1972).

after childbirth,* and then only at the beginning of a new semester.[61] Another federal court, however, struck down a board regulation which required a female employee to wait one year following delivery to gain such eligibility.[62]

Under the philosophy of the *Cohen* decision and under the EEOC guidelines requiring pregnancy and childbirth to be treated just like any other temporary disability, if the board permits an employee temporarily disabled by other physiological conditions to return to work as soon as he wishes and is medically fit to do so, it would have to treat female teachers in the same fashion following delivery.

(10.) Is a maternity leave policy which grants female teachers leave to care for an infant child but denies such leave to male teachers repugnant to the equal protection clause?

A federal court in New York has held that a "colorable constitutional claim" would be presented by such a contention. The court ruled that a male lecturer in sociology at the City University of New York was entitled to a trial on his claim that women faculty members were permitted to take a leave of absence to care for a newborn infant without adversely affecting their tenure rights, but that the same child care privilege was denied to men.[63]

(11.) Is an anti-nepotism rule which, for example, denies employment to the spouse of a teacher on the staff, or denies tenure to the spouse of a tenured teacher in the department, a violation of the equal protection clause?

Yes, if the rule discriminates on the basis of sex. Such discrimination may appear on the face of the rule. Or the rule may be discriminatory as applied in practice. Furthermore, where the effect of such a rule is to disproportion-

*The appellate court decision in *LaFleur*, handed down as this book went to press, reversed the trial court's ruling and held this provision unconstitutional since it bore no relation whatever to the employer's interests. *LaFleur* v. *Cleveland Board of Educ., appeal docketed,* No. 71-1598, (6th Cir. July 28, 1971).

ately burden women—for example, where men constitute the great majority of the faculty—the rule would appear to be a prima facie violation of Title VII and the school system, college or university involved would be required to prove that the policy was justified by business necessity and that no less drastic alternative was available which would meet the objectives of the policy.[64] It is arguable that a similar showing would have to be made under the Constitution.[65]

(12.) Can differences in the treatment accorded tenured and nontenured teachers be so arbitrary as to violate the equal protection clause?

Yes. A federal court in Georgia struck down as repugnant to the equal protection clause a school-board policy granting maternity leave to tenured teachers but denying it to untenured teachers. Noting that board regulations drew no distinction between the two categories of teachers with respect to leave for professional study, bereavement, personal illness, emergency, or military service, the court held that the policy was arbitrary and without rational basis.[66] Relying upon this decision, an Ohio federal court invalidated as a violation of the equal protection clause a policy which granted a maternity leave of absence to untenured pregnant teachers who had served three or more years in the system, but denied it to those with less than three years of service.[67]

The contention also has been advanced, but thus far rejected by the courts, that the equal protection clause invalidates a state tenure law which fails to require a hearing for a nontenured teacher facing dismissal while mandating such a hearing for a tenured teacher.[68]

(13.) Does the equal protection clause invalidate state statutes which prescribe different procedures for the dismissal of a teacher during the school year and the termination of his employment at the end of the school year?

In a North Carolina case the court rejected this contention, asserting that: "The vast difference in the conse-

quences of these two actions, insofar as the future effect
upon the teacher's professional standing and ability to
obtain employment is concerned, is ample basis for classification within the limits of the Fourteenth Amendment. . . ."[69]

**(14.) Are there other types of discrimination by school
authorities that fall under the ban of the equal protection
clause?**

Yes. School officials would violate the equal protection
clause if they unreasonably singled out a class of teachers
for special treatment. For example, a school board could
not discipline a teacher because of his political affiliation.[70]
One judge remarked that if, "for an absurd example,"
a teacher's employing agency "thought blondes were
intrinsically too frivolous for permanent employment, a
court would find it difficult to withhold its hand."[71]

Similarly, school officials cannot impose restraints upon
particular teachers that are greater than those imposed on
other teachers in the same category. In *Trister* v. *University
of Mississippi*,[72] for example, two members of the faculty
of the University of Mississippi Law School were told by
the university to stop participating in a legal-services program in the Office of Economic Opportunity designed to
provide legal services to the poor in North Mississippi. The
only reason for making a decision adverse to the two
teachers was that they wished to continue to represent
clients who tended to be unpopular. The court held that
while the university could decide not to employ any part-
time professors, or to forbid the practice of law to every
member of its faculty, it could not, consistently with the
equal protection clause, "arbitrarily discriminate against
professors in respect to the category of clients they may
represent."[73]

**(15.) Does an age ceiling for teachers violate the equal
protection clause?**

Authority is sparse on this issue. One court has rejected
the claim—advanced by a renowned philosopher, that

Fordham University denied him equal protection of the laws by withdrawing a firm offer to award him the Albert Schweitzer Chair in Humanities on the sole ground that he had passed his sixty-fifth year. Although his physical health, mental capacity, and prognosis for length and breadth of productivity were excellent, the court concluded, the teacher was "not the victim of an invidious and impermissible discrimination."[74] The court stated:

> Notwithstanding great advances in gerontology, the era when advanced age ceases to bear some reasonable statistical relationship to diminished capacity or longevity is still future. It cannot be said, therefore, that age ceilings upon eligibility for employment are inherently suspect, although their application will inevitably fall injustly [sic] in the individual case.[75]

Thus, "vindication of the exceptional individual," the court stated, "may have to attend the wise discretion of the administrator."[76]

(16.) May a state, consistently with the equal protection clause, enact a law imposing greater restraints upon teachers in one county than upon teachers in another county?

No, at least absent a showing that the classification is reasonable and, where it impinges upon an independent constitutional right, justified by a compelling state interest. Thus, a Florida law forbade all administrators and supervisors in the Palm Beach County school system to participate or become a member in any organization which engaged in collective representation of teachers with regard to terms and conditions of employment. The court held that in addition to invading basic freedoms of expression and association protected by the First and Fourteenth Amendments, the law violated the equal protection clause, stating: "The defendants have made no effort to demonstrate that Palm Beach County is in any way unique so as to justify placing its educational employees in a class apart from those of other Florida counties. Nor has any compelling state concern been shown to underly this statute."[77]

Some states confer tenure protection upon teachers in certain school districts, but exempt others, typically small rural school districts, on the ground that they would be overly burdened by the obligation to implement the tenure laws. It is questionable whether such state laws are consistent with the equal protection clause.

In one case, a three-judge federal district court held unconstitutional acts of the Alabama legislature denying benefits of the state teacher tenure law to eight counties which, with one exception, were among the twelve counties of the state having a majority black population.[78] The court held that the statutes classified on the basis of race and therefore violated the equal protection clause. The court, however, also concluded that "[s]ince teacher tenure statutes are involved, we would be compelled to reach the same conclusion without drawing an inference of racial classification,"[79] stating:

> Initially it should be recognized that teachers in general constitute a special class of special importance to our society. Their rights constitute a "constitutionally protected domain" which the courts should be especially careful to protect . . . Statutes such as these which have the potential to encroach upon the teaching profession's prerogatives, rights, and responsibilities must be carefully scrutinized; this is especially true where such statutes involve employment rights and tenure.[80]

Noting that the purposes of the tenure laws were to guarantee freedom to teach by protecting teachers from removal on unfounded charges or for political reasons and to benefit the public by assuring a more competent and efficient teaching force,[81] the court found no rational basis for the creation of a "second class" in an area "where the rights involved are of paramount importance and the greatest sensitivity."[82]

(17.) Can the discriminatory administration by school authorities of a valid policy deny equal protection of the laws?

Yes. School authorities, like other public officials, cannot apply even laws or policies fair on their face "with an evil eye and an unequal hand."[83]

In one case, a teacher in Alabama was terminated for violating a principal's "rule" forbidding male teachers to wear mustaches. The decision was based partly on the ground that the only teacher other than the plaintiff who wore a mustache was not asked to shave it off, and thus the plaintiff was denied equal protection of the laws.[84] Another court noted that inconsistent application of an age ceiling on eligibility for a state-endowed chair might violate the equal protection clause.[85]

(18.) Can discriminatory action by school officials in terminating, disciplining, or refusing to hire or promote a teacher be so arbitrary as to violate the due process clause?

Yes. The Supreme Court has recognized that "discrimination may be so unjustifiable as to be violative of due process."[86] Racial discrimination in the public schools of the District of Columbia, for example, was held by that Court to contravene the due process clause of the Fifth Amendment.[87] Another court held that where teachers were denied summer employment because they had brought suit against their school system, the standards for such employment were not applied to the plaintiffs "in an even-handed and rational fashion," in violation of the due process as well as the equal protection clauses of the Fourteenth Amendment.[88] Due process violations may also be found in other kinds of capricious discrimination by school officials, such as discrimination against Republican teachers or teachers with green eyes.

In a New York case the court, without expressly reaching any federal constitutional issue, held "arbitrary and capri-

cious" a rule denying a teacher a substitute teaching license
solely because she was overweight. The teacher had worked
for three years and satisfactorily performed her duties.
Suggesting that the Board of Examiners was applying an
"aesthetic standard," the court held that "obesity, standing
alone, is not reasonably and rationally related to the ability
to teach or to maintain discipline."[89] Responding to a
medical finding that "*all* obese persons are generally prone
to certain specified illnesses—rising blood pressure, swell-
ing of extremities, diabetes, cardiovascular ailments—all of
which may in the future lead to 'absences' and to early
retirement from service"—the court observed that "*this*
petitioner has had only two days of absence in three terms
of teaching. . . ."[90]

Subsequently, a California court held a decision not to
rehire an overweight physical-education teacher violative
of state law, and characterized as arbitrary the principal's
decision not to recommend her for re-employment, where
the evidence failed to show that her condition significantly
impaired her ability to teach.[91] Unimpressed with the
board's claim that she was unable to serve as "a model of
health and vigor," the court said: "Any requirement that
teachers exemplify the subjects they teach and embody all
of the qualities which they hope to instill in their students
would be utterly impossible of fulfillment. As for any contention that plaintiff set a bad example which her students
might imitate, it is apparent that obesity, by its very nature,
does not inspire emulation."[92]

**(19.) Are there other types of unreasonable action by
school authorities which, although not necessarily involving
either discrimination or reprisal for the exercise of a constitutional right, are so arbitrary as to violate the due
process clause?**

Yes. Although there is still some conflict among the
courts on this issue, many recent cases have held or indicated that the concept of "substantive due process" forbids
arbitrary or capricious personnel decisions by school authorities.

One federal court of appeals, for example, recognized that a "bad faith" refusal to renew a probationary teacher's contract "may rise to a constitutional level, in which case the federal courts are available. . . ."[93] It seems doubtful, for example, that the Constitution would permit the termination of a teacher's employment because she refused to submit to the improper advances of her superintendent.[94]

Thus, a federal district court refused to dismiss a complaint under the Civil Rights Act by a school nurse who alleged that the real reason for the refusal of the defendant school authorities to renew her contract was her insistence on exercising her legal right to seek a transfer. If this allegation were true, the court declared, "then a serious legal question arises whether defendants' action was not so arbitrary, unreasonable and discriminatory as to violate substantive due process."[95]

In a Delaware case, an educational secretary alleged that her employment contract was not renewed because of her husband's activities as chairman of the negotiations committee for the teachers' association. The court ruled that her complaint stated a claim upon which relief could be granted, holding that "dismissal based on another person's exercise of a constitutional right is so patently arbitrary and capricious to be a deprivation of substantive due process."[96]

(20.) Can there be a violation of substantive due process without a showing of bad faith?

Yes. The courts have made it clear, for example, that the nonrenewal of a teacher's contract can be arbitrary and capricious, and a denial of due process, even if it is not malicious but merely thoughtless. If the reason for nonrenewal, one federal court of appeals indicated, is "unrelated to the educational process or to working relationships within the educational institution," it is invalid.[97] A teacher, said the court, "may not be dismissed for the type of automobile she drives or for the kinds of foods she eats."[98]

Similarly, due process requires that a teaching qualification have more than a tenuous connection with fitness to teach. One of the grounds upon which federal courts struck down minimum cut-off score requirements on the Graduate Record Examination and the National Teachers Examination as qualifications for employment and re-employment of teachers in a public school system was that such requirements were arbitrary and unreasonable because they were not substantially related to the requirements of the job.[99]

Again, "a reason [for nonrenewal] may be arbitrary in that it is trivial."[100] In *Johnson* v. *Branch*,[101] a nontenured teacher's contract had not been renewed, allegedly because of multiple infractions of school rules. Although the court determined that the actual reason for nonrenewal was the teacher's civil rights activity, it also ruled that the infractions, ranging from arriving at school a few minutes late to arriving fifteen minutes late to supervise an evening athletic contest, were too insignificant to warrant the sanction of nonrenewal. The court held that while a school board has discretion in determining whether to renew the contract of a nontenured teacher, "[d]iscretion means the exercise of judgment, not bias or capriciousness. Thus it must be based on fact and supported by reasoned analysis."[102]

One court has stated that under the due process clause of the Fourteenth Amendment school authorities cannot refuse to reemploy a nontenured teacher "for a reason not supported by substantial evidence. . . ."[103] Other courts have held or indicated that such a refusal may not, consistently with the due process clause, "rest on a basis wholly unsupported in fact, or on a basis wholly without reason."[104] As one court stated:

> To expose him [an untenured professor] to non-retention because the deciding authority is utterly mistaken about a specific point of fact, such as whether a particular event occurred, is unjust. To expose him to non-retention on a basis wholly without reason, whether subtle or otherwise, is unjust. There can be no question that, in terms of money and standing and opportunity to contribute to the educational process,

the consequences to him probably will be serious and prolonged and possibly will be severe and permanent. 'Badge of infamy' is too strong a term, but it is realistic to conclude that non-retention by one university or college creates concrete and practical difficulties for a professor in his subsequent academic career.[105]

Based on similar considerations, a federal court invalidated the nonrenewal of a high school teacher whose employment was terminated after the superintendent and school board, on the basis of uninvestigated complaints and unverified rumors that he had made sexual advances towards female students, concluded—without any evidence —that he had "lost his effectiveness." Holding that the nonrenewal violated the teacher's right to due process, the court said:

> To dismiss a teacher on the basis of uninvestigated complaints and unverified rumors and to admit that the decision does not depend on the truth or falseness of the complaints and rumors is patently unjust, arbitrary, and capricious. If the possibility, let alone the probability of the truth of the facts involved is not known, a decision cannot be reasoned or based on substantial evidence. The implications of such a decision are frightening. It means that any student with a personal dislike for a teacher could bring his career to an end by a complaint wholly unjustified and unsubstantiated in fact. In the same sense, a malicious group in the community could start unsubstantiated rumors resulting in dismissal. Further, an administrator or another teacher bent on a personal vendetta could, by insidiously starting false rumors, bring about the dismissal of a totally innocent teacher.[106]

Another federal court, condemning for lack of substantive as well as procedural due process the dismissal of a high school teacher based on parental complaints concerning his teaching method, stated:

"[I]t is the binding duty of an administrative body to act with full information, with reason and deliberation, and with full benefit of the views of supervisors, principals and others familiar with the curriculum and teaching techniques in the schools, before denying a teacher his livelihood and professional status. It is entirely unfitting that such a board should be swayed by the hearsay remarks of persons not in possession of the facts. . . ."[107]

(21.) Is it arbitrary for a board, in deciding whether to take adverse action against a teacher, to act against the weight of the evidence before it?

No. The measure of arbitrariness or capriciousness is not the wisdom of the board's action or whether it acted in accord with the preponderance of the evidence before it, but whether a reasonable person *could have found* that the performance or conduct of the teacher demonstrated a quality inimical to the legitimate interests of the school system.[108]

(22.) Does due process require that a nontenured teacher be retained unless he has failed to comply with some previously announced standard of conduct?

No. The courts have ruled that the grounds for a university's refusal to reappoint a probationary teacher need not be limited to violations of a preannounced "code of conduct."[109] Explaining its decision, one of these courts stated that "there are an enormous number of fact situations in which the nonreappointment of an employee may be justified by highly subjective and perhaps unforeseeable considerations."[110]

On the other hand, where the school system is relying on specific alleged misconduct in terminating a nontenured teacher, and the teacher cannot reasonably be expected to be on notice that his conduct is improper, due process may require that he be warned in advance that the conduct is forbidden, particularly where the conduct arguably involves the exercise of protected constitutional rights. For example, one court found a violation of due process where a school system terminated the employment of a non-tenured teacher for wearing a beard on the job in the absence of any written or announced policy that male teachers should not wear beards in the classroom.[111]

(23.) Does due process require that nonrenewal of a nontenured teacher's contract be based upon some form of misconduct, incompetence, or inefficiency?

No. For example, where a university sought to strengthen two departments in order to comply with the standards of a regional accrediting association, its action in failing to renew the contracts of two nontenured teachers with the least service in their respective departments in order to make room for teachers with advanced degrees was upheld.[112]

NOTES

1. 344 U.S. 183, 192 (1952).
2. 350 U.S. 551, 555 (1956) (emphasis added).
3. See, e.g., Armstead v. Starkville Municipal Separate School District, 331 F.Supp. 567, 571, 574 (N.D. Miss. 1971), aff'd, No. 71-2124 (5th Cir. June 9, 1972); Baker v. Columbus Municipal Separate School District, 329 F.Supp. 706, 719 (N.D. Miss. 1971), aff'd, No. 71-2531 (5th Cir. June 30, 1972). Cf. Scott v. Macy, 349 F.2d 182, 183-84 (D.C. Cir. 1965).
4. Porcelli v. Titus, 431 R.2d 1254 (3 Cir. 1970), aff'g 302 F.Supp. 726 (D. N.J. 1969).
5. E.g., Smith v. Concordia Parish School Board, 445 F.2d 285, 286 (5th Cir. 1971); Armstead v. Starkville Municipal Separate School District, No. 71-2124 (5th Cir. June 9, 1972) pp. 10-11; Baker v. Columbus Municipal Separate School District, No. 71-2531 (5th Cir. June 30, 1972) p. 5.
6. Singleton v. Jackson Municipal Separate School District, 419 F.2d 1211, 1218 (5th Cir. 1969), cert. denied, 396 U.S. 1032 (1970). The growing body of jurisprudence dealing with the displacement of black educators in the South incident to school desegregation is beyond the purview of this book.

7. *Baker* v. *Columbus Municipal Separate School District,* No. 71-2531 (5th Cir. June 30, 1972) p. 3.
8. *Ibid.*
9. *Id.* at 6.
10. *Id.* at 4.
11. *Ibid.*
12. See *Freeman* v. *Gould Special School District,* 405 F.2d 1153, 1159 (8th Cir. 1969), *cert. denied,* 396 U.S. 843 (1970); *Council* v. *Donovan,* 40 Misc. 2d 744, 750, 244 N.Y.S.2d 199, 205 (1963).
13. *Cf. Truax* v. *Raich,* 239 U.S. 33 (1915); *Takahashi* v. *Fish & Game Comm'n,* 334 U.S. 410 (1948); *Hernandez* v. *Texas,* 347 U.S. 475 (1954).
14. *Graham* v. *Richardson,* 403 U.S. 365 (1971).
15. *Younus* v. *Shabat,* 336 F.Supp. 1137 (N.D. Ill. 1971).
16. *Cf. Reed* v. *Reed,* 404 U.S. 71, 75-76 (1971).
17. *Williams* v. *San Francisco Unified School District,* 340 F.Supp. 438, 443 (N.D. Cal. 1972). See also *Sail'er Inn, Inc.* v. *Kirby,* 95 Cal. Rptr. 329, 339, 485 P.2d 529, 539 (1971) (state law prohibiting women from serving as bartenders violates equal protection clause; strict standard of review applied because statute "limits the fundamental right of one class of persons to pursue a lawful profession," and "because classifications based on sex should be treated as suspect"); *Thorn* v. *Richardson,* 4 FEP Cases 299, 302 (N.D. Wash. 1971). See generally, *Truax* v. *Raich,* 239 U.S. 33, 41 (1915) (". . . [T]he right to work for a living in the common occupations of the community is of the very essence of the personal freedom and opportunity that it was the purpose of the [Fourteenth] Amendment to secure"); *United States* ex rel. *Robinson* v. *York,* 281 F. Supp. 8, 14 (D. Conn. 1968).
18. A forthcoming book in this series, by Susan Ross, will deal comprehensively with the rights of women and will treat this subject at greater length.
19. P.L. 92-261 §2(1), U.S. Code Congressional and Administrative News 814, (Mar. 24, 1972).
20. Sec. 703 (e), 42 U.S.C. §2000e-2.
21. In contrast to its powers in the *private* employment area, EEOC has no power to file suit in court against a public employer upon the failure of conciliation, but must refer the case to the U.S. Attorney General, who may bring a suit in which the person aggrieved has the right to inter-

vene. P.L. 92-261 §4(a), U.S. Code Congressional and Administrative News 818 (March 24, 1972).

22. 29 C.F.R. §1604 *et. seq.*, 37 Fed. Reg. 6835-37 (1972). The Office of Federal Contract Compliance of the Department of Labor has issued sex discrimination guidelines designed to promote and insure equal opportunities for all persons employed or seeking employment with Government contractors and subcontractors, without regard to sex. 41 C.F.R. §60-20. 1 *et. seq.* (1970).

23. *Griggs* v. *Duke Power Co.*, 401 U.S. 424, 433-34 (1971).

24. *Cf. Baker* v. *Columbus Municipal Separate School District*, 329 F. Supp. 706, 721 (N.D. Miss. 1971), *aff'd*, No. 71-2531 (5th Cir. June 30, 1972).

25. 29 C.F.R. §1604.2 (a) (1) (i) – (iii), 37 Fed. Reg. 6836 (1972).

26. 29 C.F.R. §1604.9 (b), (c), 37 Fed. Reg. 6837 (1972).

27. 29 C.F.R. §1604.9 (d), 37 Fed. Reg. 6837 (1972).

28. 29 C.F.R. §1604.9 (f), 37 Fed. Reg. 6837 (1972).

29. H. Beale, *Are American Teachers Free?* 384-85 (1936).

30. 29 C.F.R. §1604.4 (a), 37 Fed. Reg. 6836-37 (1972).

31. 29 C.F.R. §1604.4 (b), 37 Fed. Reg. 6836 (1972).

32. *Compare Cohen* v. *Chesterfield County School Board*, 326 F.Supp. 1159 (E.D. Va. 1971), *appeal docketed*, No. 71-1704, 4th Cir. July 27, 1971; *Williams* v. *San Francisco Unified School District*, 340 F.Supp. 438 (N.D. Cal. 1972); *Heath* v. *Westerville Board of Educ.*, Civil No. 71-379 (S.D. Ohio June 28, 1972); *In re Middletown Board of Educ.*, 56 Lab. Arb. 830 (1971); and *In re Southgate Education Association and Board of Education of the Southgate Community School District*, 57 Lab. Arb. 476 (1971) *with LaFleur* v. *Cleveland Board of Educ.*, 326 F.Supp. 1208 (N.D. Ohio 1971), *appeal docketed*, No. 71-1598, 6th Cir. July 28, 1971; *Green* v. *Waterford Board of Educ.*, Civil No. 147223 (D. Conn. April 12, 1972); *Cerra* v. *School District*, 4 FEP Cases 79 (Pa. Commonwealth Ct. Dec. 21, 1971); *cf. Schattman* v. *Texas Employment Comm'n*, 459 F. 2d 32 (5th Cir. 1972). *See generally, Love's Labors Lost: New Conceptions of Maternity Leaves*, 7 Harv. Civ. Rights–Civ. Lib. L. Rev. 260 (1972).

33. *Heath* v. *Westerville Board of Educ.*, Civil No. 71-379 (S.D. Ohio June 28, 1972) p. 4.

34. *Id.* at 4-5. *Compare Cerra* v. *School District*, 4 FEP Cases 79, 82 (Pa. Commonwealth Ct. Dec. 21, 1971).

35. *Cerra* v. *School District*, 4 FEP Cases 79 (Pa. Commonwealth Ct. Dec. 21, 1971).
36. 326 F.Supp. 1159 (E.D. Va. 1971), *appeal docketed*, No. 71-1598 (6th Cir. July 28, 1971).
37. *Id.* at 1160.
38. *Id.* at 1161.
39. *Williams* v. *San Francisco Unified School District*, 340 F.Supp. 438 (N.D. Cal. 1972). *See Monell* v. *Dep't of Social Service*, 4 FEP Cases 883 (S.D. N.Y. 1972).
40. *Williams* v. *San Francisco Unified School District*, 340 F.Supp. 438, 443 (N.D. Cal. 1972). In *Robinson* v. *Rand*, 340 F.Supp. 37, 38 (D. Colo. 1972), the court suggested another reason for application of a stringent standard in such cases. The court held that an Air Force regulation providing for immediate discharge of WAFs who became pregnant must be subjected to "strict scrutiny" since the right to marry, establish a home and bring up children are among "basic civil rights of man" and restrictions on procreation must be carefully scrutinized. Compare *Struck* v. *Secretary of Defense*, —— F.2d —— (9th Cir. 1971), discussed in *Robinson, supra*.
41. *Williams* v. *San Francisco Unified School District*, 340 F.Supp. 438, 442-43 (N.D. Cal 1972).
42. *Id.* at 446.
43. 326 F.Supp. 1208 (N.D. Ohio 1971).
44. *Id.* at 1210, 1213.
45. *Id.* at 1210.
46. *Ibid.*
47. *Id.* at 1211.
48. *Williams* v. *San Francisco Unified School District*, 340 F.Supp. 438, 446 (N.D. Cal. 1972). *See also Heath* v. *Westerville Board of Educ.*, Civil No. 71-379 (S.D. Ohio June 28, 1972) p. 4.
49. *Williams* v. *San Francisco Unified School District*, 340 F.Supp. 438, 446 (N.D. Cal. 1972).
50. *Heath* v. *Westerville Board of Educ.*, Civil No. 71-379 (S.D. Ohio June 28, 1972) p. 7. *See also Love's Labors Lost: New Conceptions of Maternity Leaves*, 7 Harv. Civ. Rights–Civ. Lib. L. Rev. 260, 275-76 (1972).
51. *Schattman* v. *Texas Employment Comm'n*, 459 F. 2d 32 (5th Cir. 1972).
52. *Id.* at 39-40.
53. *Id.* at 39.
54. *Reed* v. *Reed*, 404 U.S. 71 (1971).

55. *Williams* v. *San Francisco Unified School District*, 340 F.Supp. 438, 445 (N.D. Cal. 1972).

56. *Id.* at 445.

57. *Id.* at 449. *Cf. Robinson* v. *Rand*, 340 F.Supp. 37, 38 (D. Colo. 1972).

58. 29 C.F.R. §1604.10 (a), 37 Fed. Reg. 6837 (1972). It is not clear whether dismissal of a teacher for an unwed pregnancy would fall within this rule. Compare *Doe* v. *Osteopathic Hospital*, 333 F.Supp. 1357 (D. Kan. 1971).

59. 29 C.F.R. §1604.10 (b), 37 Fed. Reg. 6837 (1972).

60. *Ibid.*

61. *LaFleur* v. *Cleveland Board of Educ.*, 326 F.Supp. 1208, 1210 (N.D. Ohio 1971), *appeal docketed*, No. 71-1598, 6th Cir. July 28, 1971.

62. *Heath* v. *Westerville Board of Educ.*, Civil No. 71-379 (S.D. Ohio June 28, 1972) p. 8.

63. *Danielson* v. *Board of Higher Educ.*, 4 FEP Cases 885 (S.D. N.Y. April 12, 1972).

64. *Cf. Griggs* v. *Duke Power Co.*, 401 U.S. 424, 431 (1971).

65. *Cf. Baker* v. *Columbus Municipal Separate School District*, No. 71-2531 (5th Cir. June 30, 1972) p. 3.

66. *Jinks* v. *Mays*, 332 F.Supp. 254 (N.D. Ga. 1971).

67. *Heath* v. *Westerville Board of Educ.*, Civil No. 71-379 (S.D. Ohio June 28, 1972).

68. *Lucia* v. *Duggan*, 303 F.Supp. 112, 119 n. 5 (D. Mass. 1969); *DeCanio* v. *School Committee*, 260 N.E. 2d 676 (Mass. 1970), *appeal dismissed for want of jurisdiction and cert. denied*, 401 U.S. 929 (1971).

69. *Still* v. *Lance*, 279 N. C. 254, 263, 182 S.E. 2d 403, 409 (1971).

70. *See Cafeteria & Restaurant Workers Union* v. *McElroy*, 367 U.S. 886, 898 (1961); *United Public Workers* v. *Mitchell*, 330 U.S. 75, 100 (1947).

71. *Zimmerman* v. *Board of Educ.*, 38 N.J. 65, 80, 183 A. 2d 25, 33 (Weintraub, C.J., concurring).

72. 420 F. 2d 499 (5th Cir. 1969).

73. *Id.* at 504. (5th Cir. 1969).

74. *Weiss* v. *Walsh*, 324 F.Supp. 75, 77 (S.D. N.Y. 1971).

75. *Ibid.*

76. *Ibid.*

77. *Orr* v. *Thorp*, 308 F.Supp. 1369, 1372 (S.D. Fla. 1969).

78. *Alabama State Teachers Ass'n* v. *Lowndes County Board of Educ.*, 289 F.Supp. 300 (M.D. Ala. 1968).

79. *Id.* at 305.

150 THE RIGHTS OF TEACHERS

80. *Id.* at 303.
81. *Ibid.*
82. *Id.* at 305.
83. *Yick Wo* v. *Hopkins,* 118 U.S. 356, 373-74 (1886).
84. *Ramsey* v. *Hopkins,* 320 F.Supp. 477 (N.D. Ala. 1970), *modified on other grounds,* 447 F. 2d 128 (5th Cir. 1971). *Cf. Baker* v. *Columbus Municipal Separate School District,* 329 F.Supp. 706, 723 (N.D. Miss. 1971), *aff'd,* No. 71-2531 (5th Cir. June 30, 1972).
85. *Weiss* v. *Walsh,* 324 F.Supp. 75, 78 (S.D. N.Y. 1971).
86. *See Bolling* v. *Sharpe,* 347 U.S. 497, 499 (1954).
87. *Bolling* v. *Sharpe,* 347 U.S. 497 (1954).
88. *Baker* v. *Columbus Municipal Separate School District,* 329 F. Supp. 706, 723 (N.D. Miss. 1971), *aff'd,* No. 71-2531 (5th Cir. June 30, 1972).
89. *Parolisi* v. *Board of Examiners,* 55 Misc. 2d 546, 549, 285 N.Y.S. 2d 936, 940 (1967).
90. 55 Misc. at 548, 285 N.Y.S. 2d at 939.
91. *Blodgett* v. *Board of Trustees,* 1 Civ. No. 27647 (Ct. App. Cal. Sept. 23, 1971).
92. *Id.* at 15, 16.
93. *Drown* v. *Portsmouth School District,* 435 F. 2d 1182, 1187 (1st Cir. 1971), *cert. denied,* 402 U.S. 972 (1971).
94. *But see Cochran* v. *O'Dell,* 334 F.Supp. 555, 556 (N.D. Tex. 1971).
95. *Conway* v. *Alfred I. DuPont School District,* 333 F.Supp. 1217, 1220 (D. Del. 1971).
96. *Hayes* v. *Cape Henlopen School District,* Civil Action No. 4019 (D. Del. April 11, 1972) pp. 31-32.
97. *Drown* v. *Portsmouth School District,* 451 F. 2d 1106, 1108 (1st Cir. 1971).
98. *Ibid.*
99. *Armstead* v. *Starkville Municipal Separate School District,* 325 F.Supp. 560, 570 (N.D. Miss. 1971), *aff'd on other grounds,* No. 71-2124 (5th Cir. June 9, 1972); *Baker* v. *Columbus Municipal Separate School District,* 329 F.Supp. 706, 722 (N.D. Miss. 1971), *aff'd on other grounds,* No. 71-2531 (5th Cir. June 30, 1972). *Cf. Schware* v. *Board of Bar Examiners,* 353 U.S. 232, 239 (1937); *Slochower* v. *Board of Higher Educ.,* 350 U.S. 551, 558 (1956); *Dent* v. *West Virginia,* 129 U.S. 114, 124-25 (1889). Such a requirement also violates the equal protection clause since it amounts to an unreasonable classification. *Armstead* v.

Starkville Municipal Separate School District, No. 71-2124 (5th Cir. June 9, 1972) pp. 8-9.

100. *Drown* v. *Portsmouth School District,* 451 F. 2d 1106, 1108 (1st Cir. 1971).

101. 364 F. 2d 177 (4th Cir. 1966), *cert. denied,* 385 U.S. 1003 (1967).

102. *Id.* at 181.

103. *Boyce* v. *Alexis I. DuPont School District,* Civil Action No. 4141 (D. Del. April 27, 1972) p. 24.

104. *Roth* v. *Board of Regents,* 310 F.Supp. 972, 979 (W.D. Wis. 1970), *aff'd,* 446 F. 2d 806 (7th Cir. 1971), *rev'd on other grounds,* 40 U.S.L.W. 5079 (U.S. June 29, 1972); *Gouge* v. *Joint School District No. 1,* 310 F.Supp. 984, 991 (W.D. Wis. 1970). *See also Lucas* v. *Chapman,* 430 F.2d 945, 948 (5th Cir. 1970); *Drown* v. *Portsmouth School District,* 451 F.2d 1106, 1108 (1st Cir. 1971); *Holliman* v. *Martin,* 330 F.Supp. 1, 11 (W.D. Va. 1971).

105. *Roth* v. *Board of Regents,* 310 F.Supp. 972, 979 (W.D. Wis. 1970).

106. *Chase* v. *Fall Mountain Regional School District,* 330 F.Supp. 388, 399 (D. N.H. 1971).

107. *Sterzing* v. *Ft. Bend Independent School District,* Civil No. 69-H-319 (S.D. Tex. May 5, 1972) p. 14.

108. *Rozman* v. *Elliott,* 335 F.Supp. 1086, 1096 (D. Neb. 1971).

109. *Fluker* v. *Alabama State Board of Educ.,* 441 F.2d 201, 207 (5th Cir. 1971). *See Roth* v. *Board of Regents,* 310 F.Supp. 972, 983 (W.D. Wis. 1970), *aff'd,* 446 F.2d 806 (7th Cir. 1971), *rev'd on other grounds,* 40 U.S.L.W. 5079 (U.S. June 29, 1972).

110. *Fluker* v. *Alabama State Board of Educ.,* 441 F. 2d 201, 207 (5th Cir. 1971). *See also Holliman* v. *Martin,* 330 F.Supp. 1, 10-11 (W.D. Va. 1971); *Culross* v. *Weaver,* 71-C-75 (W.D. Wis. July 23, 1971).

111. *Lucia* v. *Duggan,* 303 F.Supp. 112, 118 (D. Mass. 1969). *See also Keefe* v. *Geanakos,* 418 F. 2d 359, 362 (1st Cir. 1969); *Mailloux* v. *Kiley,* 323 F.Supp. 1387, 1392 (D. Mass. 1971), *aff'd,* 448 F. 2d 1242 (1st Cir. 1971).

112. *Fluker* v. *Alabama State Board of Educ.,* 441 F. 2d 201 (5th Cir. 1971). *See also Culross* v. *Weaver,* 71-C-75 (W.D. Wis. July 23, 1971) p. 5.

VIII. Constitutional Protection of Procedural Rights

PROCEDURAL DUE PROCESS

Substantive constitutional protection for a teacher may well, as one court has suggested, be "useless without procedural safeguards."[1] Although, as a commentator has noted, a teacher "possessed of extraordinary fortitude" may elect to retain counsel to file suit, litigation entails many practical difficulties:

Faculty members are not litigious by nature, the costs of formal controversy are high and usually must be borne personally, the burden of proof—often exceedingly difficult to carry—falls upon the plaintiff-teacher, and the ordinary case may not reach judgment for months or even years after the plaintiff has been separated from his job. In addition, the teacher must face the practical recognition that the extralegal hazards of such litigation are themselves quite great: to sue and to lose establishes a public record against oneself as a teacher and may further prejudice one's chances for employment or advancement. To sue and to win will not permit one actually to resume teaching at the institution in most instances, and it will almost certainly spread upon the public record whatever evidence of the plaintiff's shortcomings the defending institution can muster—thereby warning other institutions which may be chary of seemingly irascible professors who sue their employer and "launder their linen" in public places.[2]

Absent fair procedures therefore, school authorities, motivated by unconstitutional, unlawful or improper purposes; acting upon the basis of whim or caprice, or mistaken on a point of fact, could destroy a teacher's career without any accountability for their action. Nor is this danger unreal, since a teacher occupies a vulnerable position. He may be victimized by the charge of an immature student with an imagined grievance. If he is bold or stimulating, he may be the target of outraged parents or community groups, and their zeal may be matched or exceeded by rivals or superiors in the academic community who regard him as a threat to their own security or position. The absence of fair procedures, moreover, tends to chill the exercise of constitutional rights and to discourage innovation, since few teachers will assert such rights or stray from the path of caution knowing that discharge or discipline may result with no readily available opportunity for defense.

Although they leave many questions unanswered, recent decisions of the Supreme Court shed some light upon the extent to which the due process clause of the Fourteenth Amendment requires school officials to afford procedural fairness when they seek to terminate the employment of a teacher.

(1.) Can a school board constitutionally terminate the employment of a tenured teacher without giving him the opportunity for a hearing?

No. In *Slochower* v. *Board of Higher Education*,[3] a tenured professor at a city university was dismissed under a provision of the municipal charter terminating the employment of any city employee who invoked his Fifth Amendment privilege against self-incrimination to avoid answering a question relating to his official conduct. The Supreme Court ruled:

The state has broad powers in the selection and discharge of its employees, and it may be that proper inquiry would show Slochower's continued employment to be inconsistent with a real interest of the State. But there has been no such inquiry here. We hold that the summary dismissal of appellant violates due process of law.[4]

Very recently, the Supreme Court characterized the *Slochower* decision as holding "that a public college professor dismissed from an office held under tenure provisions . . . [has an interest] in continued employment that . . . [is] safeguarded by due process."[5]

This constitutional requirement of procedural fairness is *independent* of, and may be more comprehensive than the procedural protections afforded by state tenure statutes or tenure policies of the teacher's employing institution. The requirement seems equally applicable to tenured public school teachers at the *elementary and secondary* levels. And it would appear to extend to the nonrenewal of a tenured teacher's contract as well as his dismissal during the contract term.

(2.) Can a school board constitutionally terminate the employment of a nontenured teacher without giving him the opportunity for a hearing?

In its recent decisions in *Board of Regents* v. *Roth*[6] and *Perry* v. *Sindermann*,[7] the Supreme Court ruled that the answer depends on whether the termination would deprive the teacher of "liberty" or "property." If so, he is entitled to a hearing.

In *Roth*, the Supreme Court recognized that a teacher *dismissed during the term of his contract* has a property interest safeguarded by due process.[8] Thus, any teacher—including a nontenured teacher—facing dismissal during his contract term would be entitled to a hearing under the Constitution. The court rejected the contention, however, that every nontenured teacher facing *nonrenewal of his contract* is entitled to such a hearing. Rather, the Court held, a hearing is constitutionally required in such circumstances only where the nonrenewal implicates interests in "liberty" or "property."[9]

(3.) When would a nonrenewal implicate interests in "liberty" so as to require opportunity for a hearing?

A teacher's interests in "liberty" would be implicated if the nonrenewal were based on a charge "that might seriously damage his standing and associations in his community" or if the State, in declining to rehire a teacher, imposes on him "a stigma or other disability that foreclose[s] his freedom to take advantage of other employment opportunities."[10]

(4.) When would a charge underlying nonrenewal "seriously damage a teacher's standing and associations in his community" so as to require opportunity for a hearing?

The question is open. The examples cited by the Court are charges of dishonesty or immorality.[11] Arguably, however, charges of disloyalty, incompetence, insubordination, unreliability, or other grounds casting a shadow on a teacher's reputation fall within the rule. Such charges also might constitute a "stigma" or "disability" foreclosing other employment opportunities within the meaning of the Court's decisions.[12]

(5.) Where no reasons are given for nonrenewal, what evidence is required to prove that, in declining to rehire a teacher, the State has imposed "a stigma or other disability that foreclose[s] his freedom to take advantage of other employment opportunities?"

In *Roth,* the Court indicated that this test would be satisfied by proof that incident to the nonretention of a teacher in a state university, the State invoked a regulation barring the teacher from all other public employment in state universities.[13] The Court also used language arguably suggesting that the test would be met where a "range of opportunities" is foreclosed by the nonrenewal.[14]

On the other hand, the Court stated that "[m]ere proof

. . . that . . . [a teacher's] record of nonretention in one job, taken alone, might make him somewhat less attractive to some other employers would hardly establish the kind of foreclosure of opportunities amounting to a deprivation of 'liberty'."[15] The Court also ruled that judicial "assumptions" of a "substantial adverse effect" resulting from nonretention are insufficient.[16] The Court left open the question whether *proof* of a "substantial adverse effect" is enough to demonstrate a state-imposed restriction on liberty.[17]

(6.) When could a nonrenewal implicate interests in "property" so as to require a due process hearing?

The Court's decisions in *Roth* and *Sindermann* do not clearly answer this question. The Court in *Roth* spoke of the Fourteenth Amendment's procedural protection of property as "a safeguard of the security of interests that a person has already acquired in specific benefits."[18] "To have a property interest in a benefit," the Court stated, "a person clearly must have more than an abstract need or desire for it. He must have more than a unilateral expectation of it. He must, instead, have a legitimate claim of entitlement to it."[19]

It is not clear what constitutes a "legitimate claim of entitlement" to reemployment. The Court in *Sindermann* ruled that proof by a teacher that his employing college had a *de facto* tenure policy arising from "rules and understandings, promulgated and fostered, by state officials"— entitling him to continued employment absent "sufficient cause"—would obligate the college to afford him a hearing on the nonrenewal of his contract.[20]

There may be circumstances, however, in which a teacher has a "property interest" in re-employment even though he cannot show that his employing institution has a *de facto* tenure policy. The Court in *Sindermann* suggested that a promise of continued employment absent "cause" would be implied not only from a written contract with a tenure provision but also from oral statements and conduct of the employer.[21] Thus, statements at the time of hire that the teacher can expect continued employment if his work is satisfactory would appear to be sufficient to meet the Court's "property" test.

Other arguably sufficient showings include a practice of denying renewal only for cause, or a practice of renewing the contracts of teachers with favorable evaluations or teachers who have not been reprimanded. It can also be fairly contended that a teacher has the required property interest where a state statute, or an institutional policy or custom, establishes eligibility standards for renewal or contains language from which such standards can be gleaned.[22]

Some States have "continuing contract" laws providing, for example, that all contracts of employment of public school teachers shall continue in full force and effect during good behavior and efficient and competent service and be deemed to continue for the next succeeding school year unless written notice of intention to terminate the contract is served upon the teacher by a certain date prior to the end of the school year. A strong argument can be made that such a law creates the requisite "property" interest within the meaning of the *Roth* and *Sindermann* decisions.

Prior to *Roth* and *Sindermann,* a federal court in Kansas held that a continuing contract law of this nature indicated that the legislature ". . . as a matter of public policy recognized a valuable interest by a public school teacher in the expectancy of continued employment . . . The very purpose of . . . continuing contract laws is to give recognition to a constitutionally protectible interest. This type of statute give teachers a certain degree of security in their positions and guarantees freedom to teach by protecting them from removal on unfounded charges or for political reasons or for exercising constitutionally protected rights."[23] Accordingly, the court ruled that a nontenured teacher employed for about five years was entitled to a statement of reasons and a hearing under the due process clause before his continuing contract could be terminated.

(7.) Can the employment of a nontenured teacher who has no formal contract constitutionally be terminated without opportunity for a hearing?

The answer again depends on whether, in the light of the circumstances, the teacher can be said to be deprived of "property" or "liberty" by the dismissal.

In one case, the Supreme Court ruled that the summary dismissal of a substitute teacher because she refused to sign a loyalty oath violated her procedural due process right.[24] In *Roth,* the Court characterized this decision as holding that the principle " 'proscribing summary dismissal from public employment without a hearing or inquiry required by due process' . . . applied to a teacher recently hired without tenure or a formal contract, but nonetheless with a clearly implied promise of continued employment."[25]

Interests in "liberty" as well as "property" also may be implicated by the termination of a teacher's employment, regardless of the teacher's tenure or contract status. A federal court of appeals, holding that a nontenured teacher dismissed during the middle of the school year had a due process right to a hearing, cited the "economic hardship of a summary deprivation of the source of one's livelihood" and the "awesome and potentially stigmatizing effect of mid-year termination."[26] In the Court's view, "a mid-year discharge [as compared to a nonrenewal] increases the economic hardship and renders even greater the likelihood that subsequent employment opportunities will be significantly circumscribed."[27] While it appears that the teacher in this case was under contract,[28] the logic of the decision seems applicable where a teacher who is not under contract is dismissed during the school year.

(8.) Are there circumstances in which a hearing is constitutionally required in connection with a reduction in force?

Where it can be shown that termination of a teacher's employment incident to a reduction in force would deprive him of "liberty" or "property," it can be contended with force that a hearing is constitutionally required. There are

CONSTITUTIONAL PROTECTION

many factual issues which may arise in the context of a reduction in force and which may bear on the propriety of the termination. For example, if the school authorities assert that the reduction is for economy reasons, it may be possible to show that the board is wrong in its assessment of the financial situation; that alternatives to reduction in force are available, or that the board did not follow objective standards in selecting the teachers whose employment was to be terminated.

In a recent ruling handed down prior to the *Roth* and *Sindermann* decisions, a Washington state court held that the due process clause of the Fourteenth Amendment mandated a fair hearing in connection with the nonrenewal of a large number of teachers for alleged economy reasons following the failure of two bond levies, and set aside the nonrenewals because they were effectuated "without due process of law as contemplated by the . . . Constitution of the United States" as well as state law.[29] Subsequently, the Court awarded the teachers damages and attorneys' fees.[30]

(9.) Can a school board constitutionally suspend a teacher without a hearing?

The logic of the recent Supreme Court decisions in *Roth* and *Sindermann* suggests that it cannot, at least where the teacher is tenured, under contract, or for other reasons would be deprived of "property" or "liberty" by the suspension.

In *Lafferty* v. *Carter*[31] a Wisconsin federal court struck down as a violation of due process the summary suspension, with full pay, of several tenured and nontenured professors at the University of Wisconsin and their exclusion from the campus. The professors had been suspended on the ground that their continuing presence during disruptive campus events was an immediate danger. The court ruled that the professors were entitled to reinstatement, and that, if the university wished to suspend any of the professors, he would be entitled to notice explaining how his presence on campus allegedly contributed to the danger and to a preliminary hearing either prior to the suspension or, if an emergency rendered that impractical, at the earliest practicable time following such interim suspension.

In *Lafferty* the court, citing its own previous decision making a similar ruling with respect to a student at a state university,[32] stated: "[W]ith respect to the right to procedural due process, the protection to be afforded a professor can hardly be less than that afforded a student, and probably should be greater."[33]

Special circumstances arguably might justify immediate suspension of a teacher accused of sexually assaulting a student, or of some other conduct which, if true, would pose a "clear and present danger" to the students or the school system, provided that the teacher's pay were continued and he were afforded a subsequent hearing at the earliest practicable time.[34]

(10.) Are there circumstances in which opportunity for a hearing is constitutionally required where a teacher is faced with a form of discipline other than dismissal, suspension or nonrenewal?

Yes. The logic of *Roth* and *Sindermann* would appear to require opportunity for a hearing whenever the discipline would deprive the teacher of an interest in "property" or "liberty."

If, for example, the teacher has tenure in a particular position, or a right to the position, absent a showing of cause, under an express or implied contract or under the policies or practices of the institution, his demotion to a position carrying less pay or responsibility presumably would deprive him of a "property" interest and thus could not, under the Constitution, be effectuated without a hearing. Where a nontenured junior college teacher had been employed for many years as chairman of the Psychology Department and the Faculty Handbook stated that "tenure is expected to be stable," a court ruled, prior to *Roth* and *Sindermann,* that she had an expectancy of reemployment under the policies and practices of the institution, and could not be removed from that position and placed as an instructor on probation without notice and hearing meeting procedural due process standards.[35]

Similarly, a demotion or reassignment arguably may deprive a teacher of "liberty" because it may substantially impair his standing and associations in the community or his ability to pursue his chosen profession. In another case decided before *Roth* and *Sindermann*, a teacher was removed from the classroom and assigned to a job in the school library requiring substantially less intellect and training, because of his refusal to comply with an unexplained order of the dean requiring him to submit to a psychiatric examination. The court held that the teacher had a due process right to challenge the reasonableness of the school board's charge of mental incompetency, either at a hearing on that order itself, or at a subsequent hearing when removal from the classroom was sought.[36] The court placed some emphasis upon the effect on the teacher's reputation resulting from the combination of being singled out and ordered to see a psychiatrist and his removal from teaching duties.

In one unusual case, a school board, as a condition of rescinding its acceptance of the mass resignations of teachers in the system during an educational crisis precipitated by gubernatorial vetoes and threatened vetoes of educational appropriations measures, imposed a "fine" of $100 upon each returning teacher. A federal district court ruled that the board's action violated the due process clause because, in addition to constituting an *ad hoc* imposition of a penalty for a wrong which had not been previously defined either by the board or the legislature and for which there was no legislatively specified penalty, each fine "was imposed without any process or procedure."[37]

(11.) Where a hearing is constitutionally required in connection with the termination of a teacher's employment or the discipline of a teacher, must the hearing precede the termination or discipline?

Yes. In *Roth*, the Court stated that "[w]hen protected interests are implicated the right to some kind of *prior* hearing is paramount."[38] As the Court noted: ". . . except in emergency situations [and this is not one] due process requires that when a state seeks to terminate [a protected] interest . . . , it must afford 'notice and opportunity for hearing appropriate to the nature of the case' *before* the termination becomes effective."[39]

(12.) Where a hearing is constitutionally required, what specific procedural rights does the teacher have?

In *Sindermann,* the Court held that proof of a property interest in continued employment "would obligate college officials to grant a hearing at his request, where he could be informed of the grounds for his nonretention and challenge their sufficiency."[40] In neither *Sindermann* nor *Roth,* however, did the Court shed much light on the nature of the hearing that would be required to permit a teacher adequately to challenge the sufficiency of the reasons for nonretention, except that in *Roth* the Court suggested that a "*full* . . . [as well as a "*prior*"] hearing" is necessary.[41]

In *Roth,* however, the Court made frequent reference to its prior decision in *Goldberg* v. *Kelly,*[42] where it formulated the following minimum procedural safeguards necessary to afford a fair hearing to a welfare recipient where the government proposes to terminate his benefits:

(1) the opportunity to be heard " 'at a meaningful time and in a meaningful manner' ";

(2) "timely and adequate notice detailing the reasons for a proposed termination";

(3) the opportunity to confront and cross-examine witnesses;

(4) the opportunity to present arguments and evidence orally, as well as in writing;

(5) the right to retain an attorney;

(6) a determination resting "solely on the legal rules and evidence adduced at the hearing";

(7) a statement by the decision maker of the reasons for the determination and of the evidence relied on; and

(8) an impartial decision maker.[43]

Arguably, a teacher whose employment the school authorities proposed to terminate is entitled to no less in the way of procedural protection. Like the welfare recipient whose benefits are terminated, such a teacher may well be driven, along with his family, "to the wall."[44]

Lower courts holding or assuming, prior to the decisions in *Roth* and *Sindermann,* that a hearing was constitutionally mandated in connection with the termination of a teacher's employment or the discipline of a teacher were divided on the nature of the hearing required.[45] Many courts, however, extended to teachers rights which *Goldberg* recognized in the welfare context. Other courts elaborated upon and expanded those rights.

On the issue of notice, for example, one federal court of appeals ruled that a teacher entitled to a due process hearing has the right to be advised not only "of the cause or causes for his termination in sufficient detail to fairly enable him to show any error that may exist," but also "of the names and the nature of the testimony of witnesses against him . . . ."[46] Other courts ruled that the statement of reasons must be in writing.[47] One judge expressed doubt that a teacher told in advance of a nonrenewal hearing only that "better qualified candidates are available" is given the assistance in preparing for a hearing that due process requires.[48]

Courts also have held that a teacher who is entitled to a due process hearing has the right not only to a statement of reasons but to notice of a hearing,[49] which must be held at "a reasonable time" after the teacher is apprised of the charges against him and which must accord the teacher "a meaningful opportunity to be heard in his own defense,"[50] including a "reasonable opportunity to submit evidence relevant to the stated reasons,"[51] the right to confront and cross-examine witnesses,[52] and the right to present opening and closing statements to the tribunal.[53] One court ruled that four hours notice of the hearing was insufficient to satisfy due process requirements.[54]

A federal court held that a tenured teacher was denied due process in a dismissal proceeding where witnesses for the administration testified that he was incompetent based on parental complaints located in an administrative file to which the teacher had no access.[55] And a state court—similarly relying on the Federal Constitution—held that a teacher's due process rights were violated where the board members, prior to the hearing, obtained information from the superintendent concerning each of the charges upon which dismissal was sought, and relied upon such evidence, which was not introduced at the hearing, in reaching its decision.[56]

Several courts have ruled that due process requires school authorities to give the teacher "an opportunity to be present [at the hearing] with counsel. . . ."[57] At least one court has held that counsel must be permitted to actively represent his client at the hearing.[58]

One federal court of appeals stated that the hearing must be recorded so that it can later be transcribed for judicial review.[59] A federal district court ordered a college to furnish a federally qualified court reporter to take down all proceedings at a court-ordered administrative hearing on the nonrenewal of an instructor's contract, and to make a copy available to the instructor.[60] Although one court ruled that a teacher could be required to bear the expense of obtaining a copy of the transcript absent a showing of financial inability to pay,[61] another court held that where a state statute required the school board to make and preserve a record of a nonrenewal hearing and furnish a copy to the teacher without cost, the failure of the board to comply violated the teacher's "constitutional right of due process," as well as, presumably, state law.[62]

One judge expressed concern over the failure of the hearing tribunal to state its decision following the hearing, "not to mention stating the basis for its decision," noting that "[u]nder these circumstances, it is difficult to ascertain whether the reason stated in advance of the hearing is the operative reason."[63] Another court implied that the tribunal is obligated by due process to state the grounds for its decision.[64]

It also has been held that a teacher was denied due

process where the deciding vote was cast by one who was not present at the hearing.[65] In a Washington case, a state court ruled that a board violated a provision of state law requiring a "full . . . hearing" because not every member of the board was present during all the testimony and arguments of counsel. The case involved the nonrenewal of a large number of teachers in the Renton, Washington school system following a double bond levy failure. The court said:

> However, although the crisis demanded much of the Board members, the legislative enactment required a full . . . hearing for each teacher. A full hearing would have required that each member of the Board be present during all of the testimony and arguments of counsel. This would, of course, have encroached further on the private lives of the Board members but when that prospect is balanced with the prospect that an individual will lose his or her livelihood then it is understood that the Board member must perform all the responsibilities of the office notwithstanding the impact on their personal affairs. It is not relevant that the elected official did not foresee at the time he or she ran for election that the time required would far exceed the time the Board member anticipated would be required.[66]

Although, in the quoted passage, the court relied on a provision of state law, a fair reading of the full opinion warrants the conclusion that the court was basing its holding on the due process clause of the Fourteenth Amendment as well.[67]

(13.) Where a teacher has a right to a due process hearing, does this include the right to an impartial decision-maker?

Yes. In *Goldberg* v. *Kelly*,[68] the Supreme Court held that "an impartial decison-maker is essential" to afford due process to a welfare recipient on the issue of whether his benefits should be terminated. One federal court of appeals has stated that where due process mandates a hearing in cases of teacher termination or nonrenewal, the hearing must be before a tribunal which "has an apparent impartiality toward the charges."[69] The same court subsequently indicated that the hearing should be before an "impartial official."[70]

Arguably, no school board can sit as an "impartial tribunal" with respect to the alleged derelictions of its own employees, particularly where the chief witnesses include administrators with whom the board has a close relationship and on whom it heavily relies. One court, however, has rejected the view "that the Fourteenth Amendment automatically requires that, in cases involving state or local governmental institutions such as universities, the 'tribunal' must be composed of members who are without prior knowledge of the persons and circumstances involved in the dispute."[71] Another court saw "serious problems" with requiring that a body of neutral outsiders review personnel decisions "that are properly the responsibility of the [School] Committee."[72]

This broad question must be distinguished from narrower issues involving the impartiality of the tribunal. For example, the Supreme Court has referred to the "obvious defects" in the fact-finding process where the school board was the trier of fact, the prosecutor that brought the charges aimed at securing the teacher's dismissal, and the victim of the teacher's statements that formed the basis of the charges.[73] One federal judge, in holding that the board was not the impartial tribunal required by the due process clause, relied in part on the fact that several board members appeared as witnesses against the teacher at the hearing.[74] A state court ruled that a tenured teacher was denied a fair hearing before the board of education where the tribunal's advisor also served as prosecuting attorney.[75]

Several courts have held that the due process impartiality requirement is violated if the board makes an initial decision to terminate a teacher's employment and *subsequently* holds a hearing.[76] Similarly, if the board makes known its position that the teacher's employment should be terminated and the hearing is later held before a tribunal containing an administrative officer directly responsible to the board, the tribunal lacks the requisite "apparent impartiality" since the administrator cannot be free to act as his conscience directs contrary to the expressed wishes of his employer.[77]

PRIVILEGE AGAINST SELF-INCRIMINATION

(1.) May a teacher constitutionally be dismissed because he has exercised his privilege against self-incrimination before a legislative committee or other investigatory body?

No. The Supreme Court has stated that ". . . public employees are entitled, like all other persons, to the benefit of the Constitution, including the privilege against self-incrimination."[78] A public employee may not constitutionally be "confronted with Hobson's choice between self-incrimination and forfeiting his means of livelihood. . . ."[79]

Thus, a teacher cannot constitutionally be discharged merely because he has exercised his privilege against self-incrimination before a legislative committee.[80] And where a public employee is compelled to testify under threat of removal from office, his testimony cannot be used against him in a subsequent criminal prosecution. In one case, for example, the Supreme Court upset the convictions of police officers based on their answers to questions by the state attorney general concerning alleged fixing of traffic tickets. In requiring officers to answer on pain of forfeiting their jobs, the Court ruled, the state law was unconstitutional. The Court declared: "[P]olicemen, like teachers and lawyers, are not relegated to a watered-down version of constitutional rights."[81]

(2.) Can a teacher constitutionally be discharged for refusing to waive immunity from prosecution granted in return for his testimony before a grand jury or other investigatory body?

No. A public employee may not be discharged for refusing to waive a constitutional right, including his privilege against self-incrimination. Thus, where a public employee is granted immunity from criminal prosecution in return for his testimony, he cannot constitutionally be discharged for refusing to waive such immunity.[82]

(3.) Does the privilege against self-incrimination shield from discharge a teacher who refuses to answer questions by school authorities related to the performance of his official duties?

This issue has not been clearly resolved. In one case, the Supreme Court held that a teacher could be discharged for refusing to answer his superintendent's questions concerning his loyalty and activities in allegedly subversive organizations, even though the refusal to answer was based on his Fifth Amendment privilege. In so holding, the Court said: "By engaging in teaching in the public schools, petitioner did not give up his right to freedom of belief, speech or association. He did, however, undertake obligations of frankness, candor and cooperation in answering inquiries made of him by his employing Board examining into his fitness to serve it as a public school teacher."[83]

It is not clear whether the Court would take so broad a view today of the scope of a school system's inquisitorial powers. In recent years, the Court has stated that the privilege against self-incrimination does not bar dismissal of a public employee who refuses "to answer questions *specifically, directly,* and *narrowly* relating to the performance of his official duties. . . ."[84]

In any event, before a teacher may be dismissed for refusing to account for performance of his public trust, he must be given a proper hearing.[85] Nor can he be required to waive his immunity with respect to the use of his answers or the fruits thereof in a criminal prosecution of himself.[86]

(4.) Does the privilege against self-incrimination protect from discipline a teacher who refuses to respond to a subpoena compelling his appearance before a grand jury?

No. The privilege against self-incrimination does not
shield a teacher who refuses to appear before an investigat-
ing agency.

In a New York case, for example, faculty members at
the state university were disciplined for refusing to comply
with a subpoena compelling their appearance before a
grand jury to answer questions as to whether they had ever
used drugs with students, advocated drug use to students, or
discussed such use or advocacy with the college administration. The court held that issuance of the subpoena did not
violate their Fifth Amendment rights. The court, however,
indicated that had the teachers appeared before the grand
jury but refused to answer questions, the refusal could not
be taken as the equivalent of guilt or otherwise used against
them in any way by their employer.[87]

NOTES

1. *Roth* v. *Board of Regents,* 310 F.Supp. 972, 979-80 (W.D.
   Wis. 1970), *aff'd,* 446 F.2d 806 (7th Cir. 1971), *rev'd,*
   40 U.S.L.W. 5079 (U.S. June 29, 1972). *Compare Cafeteria & Restaurant Workers Union* v. *McElroy,* 367 U.S.
   886, 900 (1961) (Brennan, J., dissenting) ("What sort of
   right is it which enjoys absolutely no procedural protection?").
2. Van Alstyne, *The Constitutional Rights of Teachers and
   Professors,* 1970 Duke L. J. 841, 859-60.
3. 350 U.S. 551 (1956).
4. *Id.* at 559.
5. *Board of Regents* v. *Roth,* 40 U.S.L.W. 5079, 5082 (U.S.
   June 29, 1972).
6. 40 U.S.L.W. 5079 (U.S. June 29, 1972).
7. 40 U.S.L.W. 5087 (U.S. June 29, 1972).
8. *Board of Regents* v. *Roth,* 40 U.S.L.W. 5079, 5082-83
   (U.S. June 29, 1972). *See Bates* v. *Hinds,* 334 F.Supp.
   528, 531-32 (N.D. Tex. 1971).
9. Prior to the decision of the Supreme Court in *Roth,* the
   federal courts had come to varying conclusions on whether
   a nontenured teacher had a right to a statement of
   reasons or a hearing upon nonrenewal of his contract.

See *Board of Regents* v. *Roth,* 40 U.S.L.W. 5079, 5080 n. 6 (U.S. June 29, 1972).

10. *Id.* at 5081.

11. *Ibid.*

12. See *Birnbaum* v. *Trussel,* 371 F.2d 672, 677 (2d Cir. 1966); *Meredith* v. *Allen County War Memorial Hospital Comm'n,* 397 F.2d 33, 35-36 (6th Cir. 1968); *Boulware* v. *Battaglia,* 327 F.Supp. 368, 375 (D. Del. 1971).

13. *Board of Regents* v. *Roth,* 40 U.S.L.W. 5079, 5081(U.S. June 29, 1972).

14. *Ibid.*

15. *Id.* at 5082 n.13.

16. *Ibid.*

17. *Ibid.*

18. *Id.* at 5082.

19. *Ibid.* See also *Weber* v. *Highway Comm'n,* 333 F.Supp. 561, 563 (D. Montana 1971).

20. *Perry* v. *Sindermann,* 40 U.S.L.W. 5087, 5090 (U.S. June 29, 1972). See *Zimmerer* v. *Spencer,* Civil Action No. 60-H-804 (S.D. Tex. March 24, 1972) p. 1.

21. *Perry* v. *Sindermann,* 40 U.S.L.W. 5087, 5090 (U.S. June 29, 1972). See *McFerren* v. *County Board of Educ.,* 455 F. 2d 199, 201 (6th Cir. 1972).

22. *Perry* v. *Sindermann,* 40 U.S.L.W. 5087, 5089-90 (U.S. June 29, 1972).

23. *Endicott* v. *Van Petten,* 330 F.Supp. 878, 882 (D. Kan. 1971). The question may also be raised whether a continuing contract law which simply provides that a teacher's contract remains in force absent express notice to the contrary by a date certain, but which does not expressly specify any standards which a teacher must meet to be retained, confers the "property interest" required by *Roth* and *Sindermann* to invoke the hearing requirement. Circumstances surrounding the teacher's employment, including written policies of the board and understandings fostered by school authorities, may add weight to such a contention.

24. *Connell* v. *Higgenbotham,* 403 U.S. 207 (1971).

25. *Board of Regents* v. *Roth,* 40 U.S.L.W. 5079, 5082 (U.S. June 29, 1972). Compare *Thomas* v. *Kirkwood Community College,* 448 F. 2d 1253 (8th Cir. 1971).

26. *Cooley* v. *Board of Educ.,* 453 F. 2d 282, 286 (8th Cir. 1972).

27. *Ibid. See also Schreiber* v. *Joint School District No. 1,* 335 F.Supp. 745, 749 (E.D. Wis. 1972); *Bates* v. *Hinds,* 334 F.Supp. 528, 533 (N.D. Tex. 1971).
28. *Cooley* v. *Board of Educ.,* 327 F.Supp. 454, 455 (E.D. Ark. 1971).
29. *Boyle* v. *Renton School District No. 403,* No. 740848 (Super. Ct. Wash., King County, May 1, 1972) p. 11.
30. *Boyle* v. *Renton School District No. 403,* No. 740848 (Super. Ct. Wash., King County, July 10, 1972) pp. 25, 27.
31. 310 F.Supp. 465 (W.D. Wis. 1970).
32. *Stricklin* v. *Board of Regents,* 297 F.Supp. 416 (W.D. Wis. 1969), *appeal dismissed as moot,* 420 F. 2d 1257 (1970).
33. *Lafferty* v. *Carter,* 310 F.Supp. 465, 470 (W.D. Wis. 1970).
34. *But see Moore* v. *Knowles,* 333 F.Supp. 53, 57 (N.D. Tex. 1971).
35. *Zimmerer* v. *Spencer,* No. 69-H-804 (S.D. Tex. March 24, 1972).
36. *Stewart* v. *Pearce,* No. C-70-2441 RFP (N.D. Cal. Mar. 5, 1971). *Compare Springston* v. *King,* 340 F.Supp. 314, 319-20 (W.D. Va. 1972).
37. *National Education Association* v. *Lee County Board of Public Instruction,* 299 F.Supp. 834, 840 (M.D. Fla. 1969), *certified to Florida Supreme Court,* 448 F. 2d 451 (5th Cir. 1971). The Florida Supreme Court subsequently ruled that the board's action did not violate state law, 260 So. 2d 206 (Sup. Ct. Fla. 1972), and the case is pending once more in the U.S. Court of Appeals for the Fifth Circuit, which has yet to rule on the federal constitutional issue.
38. *Board of Regents* v. *Roth,* 40 U.S.L.W. 5079, 5080 (U.S. June 29, 1972) (emphasis added).
39. *Id.* at 5080 n. 7 (emphasis added), quoting *Bell* v. *Burson,* 402 U.S. 535, 542 (1971).
40. *Perry* v. *Sindermann,* 40 U.S.L.W. 5087, 5090 (U.S. June 29, 1972).
41. *Board of Regents* v. *Roth,* 40 U.S.L.W. 5079, 5081-82 (U.S. June 29, 1972) (emphasis added).
42. 397 U.S. 254 (1970).
43. *Id.* at 267-71.
44. *Compare Sniadach* v. *Family Finance Corp.,* 395 U.S. 337, 341-42 (1969). *See also Ricucci* v. *United States,* 425 F. 2d 1252, 1956-57 (Ct. Cl. 1970) (concurring opinion) (likening the public employee whose employment is ter-

172   THE RIGHTS OF TEACHERS

minated to the welfare recipient in *Goldberg* v. *Kelly, supra*).

45. *Compare, e.g., Ferguson* v. *Thomas*, 430 F. 2d 852, 856 (5th Cir. 1970) *with Roth* v. *Board of Regents*, 310 F. Supp. 972, 980 (W.D. Wis. 1970), *aff'd*, 446 F. 2d 806 (7th Cir. 1971), *rev'd*, 40 U.S.L.W. 5079 (U.S. June 29, 1972) and *Hopkins* v. *Board of Educ.*, 330 F.Supp. 555, 559 (N.D. Ill. 1971).

46. *Ferguson* v. *Thomas*, 430 F. 2d 852, 856 (5th Cir. 1970). *See also Zimmerer* v. *Spencer*, Civil Action No. 69-H-804 (S.D. Tex. March 24, 1972) p. 3; *Bates* v. *Hinds*, 334 F. Supp. 528, 532 (N.D. Tex. 1971). *Compare Roth* v. *Board of Regents*, 310 F.Supp. 972, 980 (W.D. Wis. 1970); *Gouge* v. *Joint School District No. 1*, 310 F.Supp. 984, 992 (W.D. Wis. 1970).

47. *Bates* v. *Hinds*, 334 F.Supp. 528, 532 (N.D. Tex. 1971); *Poddar* v. *Youngstown State University*, No. C 71-227 (N.D. Ohio April 8, 1971). *Compare Henson* v. *City of St. Francis*, 322 F.Supp. 1034, 1038 (E.D. Wis. 1970).

48. *Culross* v. *Weaver*, No. 71-C-75 (N.D. Ohio July 23, 1971) p. 5.

49. *E.g., Roth* v. *Board of Regents*, 310 F.Supp. 972, 980 (W.D. Wis. 1970); *Gouge* v. *Joint School District No. 1*, 310 F.Supp. 984, 992 (W.D. Wis. 1970).

50. *Ferguson* v. *Thomas*, 430 F. 2d 852, 856 (5th Cir. 1970).

51. *Roth* v. *Board of Regents*, 310 F.Supp. 972, 980 (W.D. Wis. 1970); *Poddar* v. *Youngstown State University*, No. C 71-227 (N.D. Ohio April 8, 1971) p. 2; *Ehm* v. *Fletcher*, SA-71-CA-77 (W.D. Tex. Oct. 14, 1971) p. 4.

52. *Sindermann* v. *Perry*, 430 F. 2d 939, 944 (5th Cir. 1970), *aff'd*, 40 U.S.L.W. 5087 (U.S. June 29, 1972); *Poddar* v. *Youngstown State University*, No. C 71-227 (N.D. Ohio April 8, 1971) p. 2; *Ehm* v. *Fletcher*, SA-71-CA-77 (W.D. Tex. Oct. 14, 1971) p. 4.

53. *Ehm* v. *Fletcher*, SA-71-CA-77 (W.D. Tex. Oct. 14, 1971) p. 4.

54. *Bates* v. *Hinds*, 334 F.Supp. 528, 532-33 (N.D. Tex. 1971).

55. *Johnson* v. *Angle*, 341 F.Supp. 1043, 1045, 1053 (D. Neb. 1971).

56. *Doran* v. *Board of Educ.*, Case No. 1271-A-266 (Ct. App. Ind. June 5, 1972) pp. 6, 9, 13. *See also Boyle* v. *Renton School District No. 403*, No. 740848 (Super. Ct. Wash., King County, May 1, 1972) pp. 7, 11.

57. *Poddar* v. *Youngstown State University*, No. C 71-227 (N.D.

Ohio April 8, 1971) p. 2. *See also Sindermann* v. *Perry,* 430 F. 2d 939, 944 n. 9 (5th Cir. 1970); *Ehm* v. *Fletcher,* SA-71-CA-77 (W.D. Tex. Oct. 14, 1971) p. 4. *But see Toney* v. *Reagan,* 326 F.Supp. 1093, 1098 (N.D. Cal. 1971).

58. *Ortwein* v. *Mackey,* No. 71-523˙Civ. T (M.D. Fla. Dec. 2, 1971) pp. 3-4.

59. *Sindermann* v. *Perry,* 430 F. 2d 939, 944 (5th Cir. 1970).

60. *Ehm* v. *Fletcher,* SA-71-CA-77 (W.D. Tex. Oct. 14, 1971) pp. 4-5.

61. *Toney* v. *Reagan,* 326 F.Supp. 1093, 1100 (N.D. Cal. 1971).

62. *Appler* v. *Mountain Pine School District,* HS 71-C-16 (W.D. Ark. May 30, 1972) p. 12.

63. *Culross* v. *Weaver,* 71-C-75 (W.D. Wis. July 23, 1971) pp. 5-6.

64. *Johnson* v. *Angle,* 341 F.Supp. 1043, 1048 (D. Neb. 1971).

65. *McDonough* v. *Kelly,* 329 F.Supp. 144, 150 (D. N.H. 1971).

66. *Boyle* v. *Renton School District No. 403* (Super Ct. Wash., King County, May 1, 1972) p. 7.

67. *See id.* at pp. 3-4, 6, 11.

68. 397 U.S. 254, 271 (1970).

69. *Ferguson* v. *Thomas,* 430 F. 2d 852, 856 (5th Cir. 1970); *Sindermann* v. *Perry,* 430 F. 2d 939, 9·14 (5th Cir. 1970), *aff'd,* 40 U.S.L.W. 5087 (U.S. June 29, 1972).

70. *McDowell* v. *State of Texas,* No. 30363 (5th Cir. May 6, 1971) pp. 12-13. *See also Auerbach* v. *Trustees of the California State Colleges,* 330 F.Supp. 808, 811 (C.D. Cal. 1971).

71. *Culross* v. *Weaver,* 71-C-75 (W.D. Wis. July 23, 1971) pp. 6-7.

72. *Beattie* v. *Roberts,* 436 F.2d 747, 751 (1st Cir. 1971). *See also Drown* v. *Portsmouth School District,* 435 F.2d 1182, 1186-87 (1st Cir. 1970), *cert. denied* 402 U.S. 972 (1971).

73. *Pickering* v. *Board of Educ.,* 391 U.S. 563, 578-79 n.2 (1968).

74. *Smith* v. *Sessions,* Civil Action No. 1684 (S.D. Ga. Feb. 21, 1972) p. 5.

75. *Miller* v. *Board of Educ.,* 51 Ill. App. 2d 20, 200 N.E. 2d 838 (1964). *Cf. Mack* v. *Florida State Board of Dentistry,* 296 F.Supp. 1259 (S.D. Fla. 1969), *aff'd in part,* 430 F.2d 862 (5th Cir. 1970); *State* ex rel. *Ball* v. *McPhee,* 94 N.W.2d 711, 721-22 (Wis. 1959).

76. *Zimmerer* v. *Spencer*, Civil Action No. 69-H-804 (S.D. Tex. April 13, 1972) pp. 1-3; *Boyle* v. *Renton School District No. 403* (Super. Ct. Wash., King County, May 1, 1972) pp. 3-4. *See Culross* v. *Weaver*, 71-C-75 (W.D. Wis. July 23, 1972) pp. 6-7; *Smith* v. *Sessions*, Civil Action No. 1684 (S.D. Ga. Feb. 21, 1972) p. 5. *But see Beattie* v. *Roberts*, 436 F. 2d 747, 750-51 (1st Cir. 1971); *Toney* v. *Reagan*, 326 F.Supp. 1093, 1099 (N.D. Cal. 1971).
77. *Duke* v. *North Texas State University*, 338 F.Supp 990, 995 (E.D. Tex. 1971).
78. *Uniformed Sanitation Men Ass'n* v. *Commissioner of Sanitation*, 392 U.S. 280, 284-85 (1968).
79. *Gardner* v. *Broderick*, 392 U.S. 273, 277 (1968).
80. *Slochower* v. *Board of Higher Educ.*, 350 U.S. 551 (1956).
81. *Garrity* v. *New Jersey*, 385 U.S. 493, 500 (1967).
82. *Gardner* v. *Broderick*, 392 U.S. 273 (1968); *Uniformed Sanitation Men Ass'n* v. *Commissioner of Sanitation*, 392 U.S. 280 (1968).
83. *Beilan* v. *Board of Public Educ.*, 357 U.S. 399, 405 (1958). *See also Lerner* v. *Casey*, 357 U.S. 468, 475-77 (1958); *Nelson* v. *County of Los Angeles*, 362 U.S. 1, 8 (1960).
84. *Gardner* v. *Broderick*, 392 U.S. 273, 278 (1968) (emphasis added).
85. *Slochower* v. *Board of Higher Educ.*, 350 U.S. 551, 559 (1956); *Uniformed Sanitation Men Ass'n* v. *Commissioner of Sanitation*, 392 U.S. 280, 285 (1968).
86. *Gardner* v. *Broderick*, 392 U.S. 273, 278 (1968).
87. *Boikess* v. *Aspland*, 24 N.Y. 2d 136, 299 N.Y.S. 2d 156, 247 N.E. 2d 135 (1969).

Conclusion

It is clear from this review that much of the development in the law dealing with the constitutional rights of teachers has occurred within the last few years. As teachers become increasingly more willing to challenge questionable practices by school authorities—practices which they had once accepted without question in a more paternal era—this body of law is likely to continue to grow rapidly. In the process, answers will begin to emerge to questions which have not been answered, as well as to issues which have not been posed, in this volume.

Selected Bibliography

1. R. Chanin, *Protecting Teacher Rights: A Summary of Constitutional Developments* (1970).
2. R. Chanin, *The Right of a Teacher to Hold Elected Office* (1971) (Office of Government Relations and Citizenship, National Education Association).
3. *Developments in the Law—Academic Freedom,* 81 Harv. L. Rev. 1045 (1968).
4. *Dismissal of Teachers for Cause,* 22 Am. Jur. *Proof of Facts* 563-792 (1969).
5. N. Dorsen, *The Rights of Americans,* 546-71 (1971).
6. T. Emerson, D. Haber, and N. Dorsen, *Political and Civil Rights in the United States,* 902-1041 (Little, Brown & Co. 1967).
7. *Love's Labors Lost: New Conceptions of Maternity Leaves,* 7 Harv. Civ. Rights-Civ. Lib. L. Rev. 260 (1972).
8. Natl. Educ. Ass'n Research Div., *Teacher Tenure and Contracts* (1971).
9. Natl. Educ. Ass'n Research Div., *Statutory Hearing Rights of Nontenured Teachers,* 41 NEA Research Bull. 17 (1971).
10. Van Alstyne, *The Constitutional Rights of Teachers and Professors,* Duke L. J. 841-79 (1970).

DAVID RUBIN is Deputy General Counsel of the National Education Association and also serves as counsel to NEA's DuShane Emergency Fund—a fund established for the protection of the rights of teachers. Prior to his association with the NEA, Rubin was on the staff of the Civil Rights Division of the U.S. Justice Department and later became Deputy General Counsel and Acting General Counsel of the U.S. Commission on Civil Rights.